M000282312

DAYS

40 DAYS

Encountering Jesus Between the Resurrection and Ascension

ALTON GANSKY

Nashville, Tennessee

© 2007 by Alton Gansky
All rights reserved
Printed in the United States of America

ISBN: 978-0-8054-3090-5

Published by B & H Publishing Group
Nashville, Tennessee

Dewey Decimal Classification: 232.97
Subject Headings: JESUS CHRIST—APPEARANCES

Unless otherwise noted, Scripture passages are from the Holman Christian Standard Bible, copyright © 1999, 2000, 2002, 2003 by Holman Bible Publishers, Nashville, Tennessee; all rights reserved.

Italic text in Bible verses indicates the author's emphasis.

07 08 09 10 11 10 9 8 7 6 5 4 3 2 1

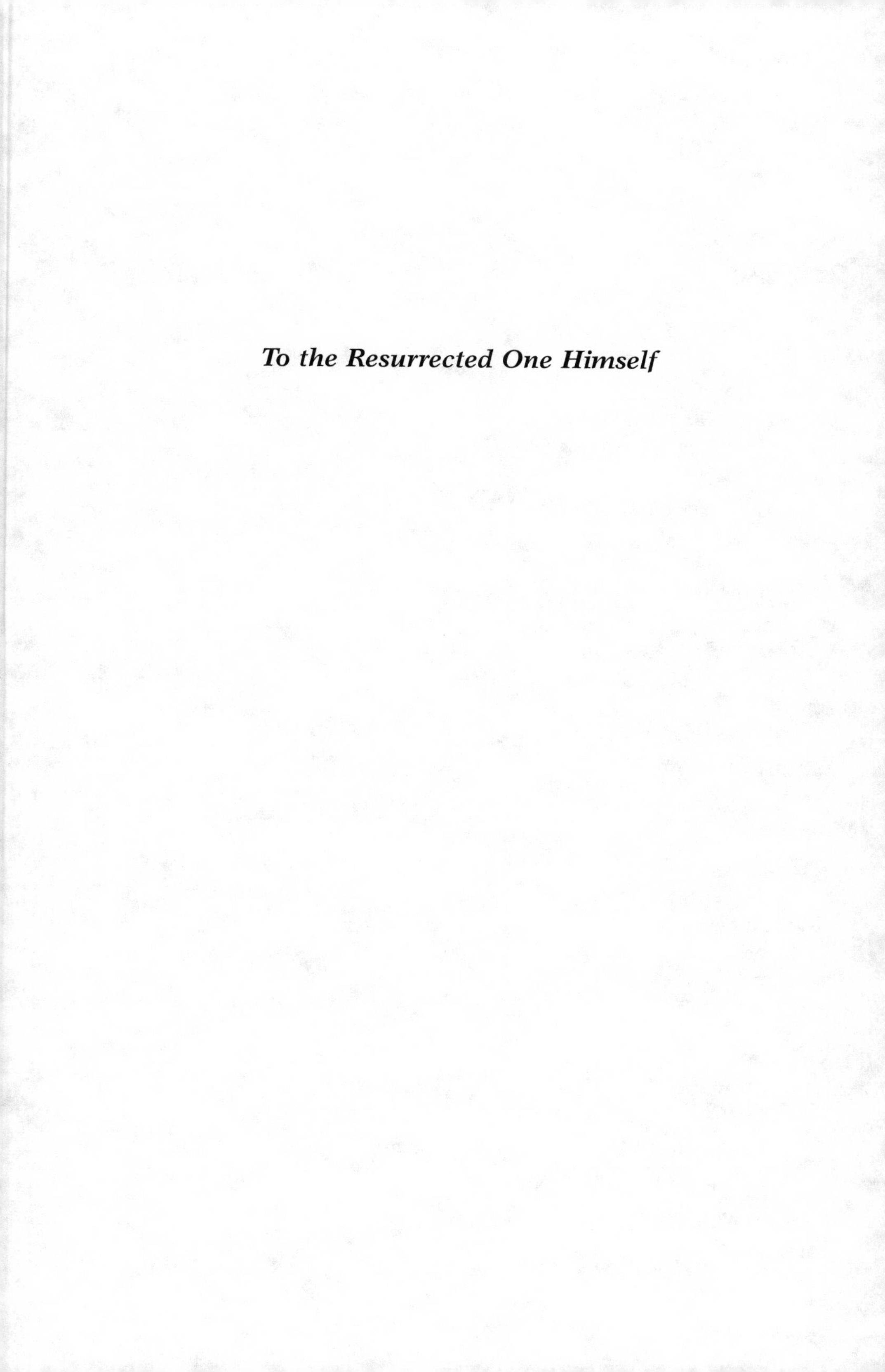

To the Resurrected One Himself

Contents

Acknowledgments ix

Part 1: **From the Cross to the Tomb**

Chapter 1: *Close Encounters of the Jesus Kind* 3
Chapter 2: *In Despair's Garden* 7
Chapter 3: *The Death Jesus Died* 23
Chapter 4: *From Wood Cross to Stone Tomb* 43
Chapter 5: *The Enigmatic Tomb* 53

Part 2: **From the Tomb to the World**

Chapter 6: *Encounter with Mary* 75
Chapter 7: *The Women Came First* 87
Chapter 8: *Peter's Secret Meeting* 101
Chapter 9: *On the Road with Jesus* 113
Chapter 10: *The Unexpected Guest* 125
Chapter 11: *The Odd Man Out* 137
Chapter 12: *Mountaintop Experience* 151
Chapter 13: *Breakfast by the Sea* 163
Chapter 14: *A Family Visit* 173
Chapter 15: *The Big Exit* 183
Chapter 16: *An Interrupted Journey* 193

***Part 3:* Never the Same**

Chapter 17: *With the Greatest Confidence* 213
Chapter 18: *The New Jesus* 225
Chapter 19: *Who Did the Raising?* 239
Chapter 20: *The Difference It Makes* 245
Chapter 21: *An Under-this-world Appearance* 259
Chapter 22: *Can This Be True?* 267

Notes 275

Acknowledgments

I wish to thank the fine people at B & H Publishing Group for their continued support and belief in this project. Special thanks go to Len Goss and Lisa Parnell, professionals who make my job much easier. Any author who undertakes a work like this is indebted to scholars, researchers, language experts, commentators, and theologians, who through the decades have created a body of work that makes a book like this possible. In a letter to Robert Hooke in 1676, the great mathematician and physicist Isaac Newton said, "If I have seen farther, it is by standing on the shoulders of giants." I am thankful to God for the giants who have come before and the giants who study for his name today, those who make it easier for us to see farther.

—Alton Gansky

Part 1

From the Cross to the Tomb

"As for Me, if I am lifted up from the earth
I will draw all [people] to Myself."
He said this to signify what kind of death
He was about to die.

—JOHN 12:32–33

There are some who would have Christ cheap.
They would have Him without the cross.
But the price will not come down.

—ATTRIBUTED TO SAMUEL RUTHERFORD

Chapter 1

Close Encounters of the Jesus Kind

In 1977, Steven Spielberg released his movie *Close Encounters of the Third Kind.* I recognized the topic the moment I heard the title. As a child and through my young adult years, I followed tales of UFOs and alien visitation. While I don't believe that aliens from another planet are vacationing on Earth, I still find the topic interesting and entertaining.

The movie title stems from a set of definitions established by famed UFO researcher J. Allen Hynek. It was his way of distinguishing one type of sighting from another and classifying them for research. He decided there were three encounter types: first kind, second kind, and third kind.

Basic sightings he called encounters of the first kind and included everything from seeing an unidentifiable light in the sky to having a clear observation of a flying saucer. A close encounter of the second kind involved physical evidence left behind by an alien spacecraft: debris, scorch marks, a depression in the ground, and so on. An encounter of the third kind involved actual contact with beings from beyond our planet. That was what Spielberg portrayed in his movie.

Through the ages, sightings of the unusual have fascinated people. During the Middle Ages in Europe and Asia it was dragons; in recent times, the Loch Ness monster, Lake Okanagan creature Ogopogo, bigfoot, yeti, aliens, UFOs, ghosts, chupacabra, leprechauns, trolls, and dinosaurs in Africa. Researchers write books and film documentaries, but these critters stay elusive and slippery.

Two thousand years ago, there were sightings of a different nature. These did not involve visitors from other planets but a divine "visitor." Jesus walked among the people of his day, was arrested and brutally killed. Three days later, he rose from the dead, appearing to chosen witnesses over a period of forty days. While sightings of lake monsters and flying saucers might be interesting, the sighting of Jesus was life changing. It is not hyperbole to state that the very core of Christianity hinges on the resurrection of Christ.

In the spring of every year, churches celebrate Easter. People who avoid church the other fifty-one weeks often attend on that special day. Preachers rise to their pulpits and proclaim the importance of the Resurrection and the hope it provides.

Then things go back to normal.

The Resurrection is one of the most written about topics in literature, with most books focusing on apologetics—the defense of the faith. Often overlooked, however, is what happened after the Resurrection. Jesus appeared a dozen times and did so in an undeniable and physical way. Bible scholars often cite these events as proof of the Resurrection, but detailed study and application of each occurrence go untapped.

Those who saw the resurrected Savior had a close encounter of the spiritual kind. They became eyewitnesses to the greatest event in history and were never the same again. Their experience changed them, and it changes us two hundred decades later.

While we need books that demonstrate the historical fact of the Resurrection, we also need one that hovers over each post-Resurrection event and ponders the event, gleaning as much as possible from the accounts. This book is an attempt to do just that.

It is my hope that by visiting each close encounter, our own daily encounter with Christ will grow more meaningful. The Resurrection is about victory over death; Resurrection encounters are about victory over doubt and despair. We will look at each appearance and glean as much truth as we can. At times we focus on key words in the text; at other times we will focus on the players in each event. In all cases we strive to see Jesus raised and the lesson each encounter teaches.

This book is for the person in the pew. I have not designed it to be a scholarly treatment, although scholarship was used in its preparation. The work intends to open doors of insight and understanding about the amazing events that followed the moment Jesus walked out of that borrowed tomb.

These pages are not necessarily an attempt to prove the Resurrection. That has been done time and time again in many fine books. We begin this journey with the belief that Christ's bodily resurrection is a fact. Our focus is on how that fact changed the eyewitnesses, the people who had a close encounter of the Jesus kind.

Chapter 2

In Despair's Garden

It is difficult to watch someone suffer.

The world was rocked by video footage of tsunamis that pounded the shores of a dozen countries and left behind more than 150,000 dead (some estimates run as high as 300,000). As hard as it was to view the destruction left by the waves, it was even more grueling to watch the images of men, women, and children struggling to survive as tons of water swept them first inland and then pulled many out to sea. They kicked, reached, struggled, and cried out for help, but nothing could be done. To watch the video was to watch people die. Once seen, those images are forever branded in our memories. We can't help but be moved by them.

During my years as a pastor, I often visited hospital bedsides of my parishioners. Most of the time I saw people who were sick or recuperating from surgery. They looked pained and uncomfortable, but it was a sight ministers get used to. Some situations, however, were far more taxing, more heartrending.

I walked into the hospital to visit a man who had been having a rough go of life. For weeks he lay in the hospital, his body ravaged by unforgiving diabetes. The doctors were valiant in their efforts, bringing to bear the best that medicine had to offer. It did no good. Before long, my friend had surgery that removed both of his legs. The image of him in bed is still vivid. Years have done nothing to blur the memory. He was in pain and remained in pain until he died. Despite morphine, he would moan in his sleep. He was a great soul, full of life and humor and possessing the kindest heart I have known.

His pain became pain for his family and friends. They are images that will never be erased.

To understand the resurrection and the appearances of Christ after his crucifixion, we must first see his death, and not just his death but his suffering. Like the tsunami video, like the hospital room of my friend, they are hard images to view, and the desire to close the book and watch television is understandable. Even so, the glory of the resurrection is built on the horror of Christ's death. To appreciate the former, we must examine the latter.

It was a dark road that led to the glory of the empty tomb.

Four Gospels, One Story

For a long time, I took my image of Christ in the Garden of Gethsemane from paintings such as the one by the nineteenth-century artist Heinrich Hofmann. His rendering shows Jesus kneeling at a large, flat stone, his fingers interlaced and his face directed heavenward with an expression of quiet reflection. Other paintings have followed suit, portraying Jesus in the dark of a Jerusalem night, kneeling in somber prayer.

The Gospels, four books in the New Testament, paint a different picture, one that is less pleasant and serene. In the first three Gospels we get a clear picture of what took place that dark night two millennia ago.

Gospel means "good news." It refers to an announcement by a messenger that was a pleasure to hear and a joy to give. These four Gospels bear the names of their human authors: Matthew, Mark, Luke, and John. The first three are often called the synoptic Gospels. Synoptic means to "see together." They are similar in the accounts they contain and in the way they portray Jesus. John's Gospel is very different in approach, making it stand out from the others.

When I was in college and graduate school, my professors spoke of the Synoptic Problem. By that they meant the factual variations in the accounts. One Gospel might say that Jesus freed two men possessed by demons (Matt. 8:28–34) while parallel accounts mention only one man (Mark 5:1–20; Luke 8:26–39). It took me a long time to come to terms with the Synoptic Problem. It was nettlesome and implied that something was wrong with the accounts—that Luke got something right that Matthew got wrong. For someone who believed the Bible to be inspired by God, such thinking was unpalatable.

Over years of Bible study, I came to understand the Synoptic Problem isn't a problem at all. The variations in historical accounts weren't errors but *enhancements.* I began to study the Gospels together, reading from a Gospel parallel that laid the three synoptic Gospels side by side so I could compare them.

That's what we are about to do. We are going to look at Gethsemane through the eyes of the different Gospel writers and in doing so, see the big picture in all its detail.

Let's Back Up for a Minute

One of the great oddities of the Bible is that John, a disciple of Christ numbered among the three allowed to go into the garden while Jesus prayed, recorded nothing of the event. In his Gospel he mentioned their crossing of the Kidron Valley and entrance into the garden but nothing more. The next verse skips to the arrival of Judas and the mob.

Shouldn't there be more? Why skip such a crucial, heart-rending scene? When we lay John's Gospel alongside the others, we see he left out many things: Jesus' genealogy, birth, baptism, the temptations, exorcisms, Christ's transfiguration, the Last Supper, and the Ascension. More than 90 percent of John's Gospel is original material.[1] His goal was not to repeat what had already been reported but to add material that completed the picture. Perhaps that is why the last line of the book that bears his name reads, "And there are also many other things that Jesus did, which, if they were written one by one, I suppose not even the world itself could contain the books that would be written" (John 21:25).

Still, omitting two key events that he was one of three select men to witness seems odd. Perhaps it was because John preferred the background to the limelight. To be one of the select three was heady stuff. In John's defense, the other two disciples did not mention the event either. Peter did, however, allude to the Mount of Transfiguration in one of his two letters (2 Pet. 1:17–18). (Most scholars believe Peter was the apostle behind the Gospel of Mark.)

Perhaps the answer lies in the simplest explanation—they missed most of the ordeal. Each of the three synoptic Gospels records that Jesus left his disciples, traveled a number of yards away, and collapsed in prayer. When he returned to the select three, he found them sleeping. Of the three, only Peter is addressed directly. "Then He came and found them sleeping. 'Simon, are you sleeping?' He asked Peter. 'Couldn't you stay awake one hour?'" (Mark 14:37).

What Jesus went through, he went through alone.

Instant Agony

In a lonely garden lit by an ivory moon, Jesus started down the path of soul-shredding anguish. According to John, Jesus had already tasted what was to come. In John 12 rests an account easy to miss.

> Now some Greeks were among those who went up to worship at the festival. So they came to Philip, who was from Bethsaida in Galilee, and requested of him, "Sir, we want to see Jesus."
>
> Philip went and told Andrew; then Andrew and Philip went and told Jesus. Jesus replied to them, "The hour has come for the Son of Man to be glorified.
>
> "I assure you: Unless a grain of wheat falls into the ground and dies, it remains by itself. But if it dies, it produces a large crop. The one who loves

his life will lose it, and the one who hates his life in this world will keep it for eternal life. If anyone serves Me, he must follow Me. Where I am, there My servant also will be. If anyone serves Me, the Father will honor him.

"Now My soul is troubled. What should I say—Father, save Me from this hour? But that is why I came to this hour. Father, glorify Your name!"

Then a voice came from heaven: "I have glorified it, and I will glorify it again!"

The crowd standing there heard it and said it was thunder. Others said, "An angel has spoken to Him!"

Jesus responded, "This voice came, not for Me, but for you. Now is the judgment of this world. Now the ruler of this world will be cast out. As for Me, if I am lifted up from the earth I will draw all people to Myself." He said this to signify what kind of death He was about to die.

Then the crowd replied to Him, "We have heard from the law that the Messiah will remain forever. So how can You say, 'The Son of Man must be lifted up'? Who is this Son of Man?"

Jesus answered, "The light will be with you only a little longer. Walk while you have the light so that darkness doesn't overtake you. The one who walks in darkness doesn't know where he's going. While you have the light, believe in the light so that you may become sons of light." Jesus said this, then went away and hid from them. (vv. 20–36)

A group of Greeks requested a meeting with Jesus. They approached the disciple Philip (*Philip* is a Greek name that means "lover of horses.") This was not an uncommon occurrence. The way to speak to a teacher was always through his students. That custom was carried out in Jesus' day. Philip delivered the request but Jesus ignored it. We don't know what happened to the Greeks. Instead of agreeing or refusing to grant the audience, Jesus started down a different path with a whiplash change in direction.

He spoke with boldness about events he knew well and the world would soon understand. His glory was not far off. Strange choice of word—*glory.* Jesus spoke of his death—and an ugly death it was going to be—but he called it his "glory." The word (*doxazo*) he used means to magnify and to esteem—to be recognized and honored. Remember, he was talking about his execution on the cross.

Jesus followed that with a brief lesson about how death led to life, how a kernel of grain could lead to a harvest of crops. But then storm clouds rolled in like a hurricane: "Now My soul is troubled. What should I say—Father, save Me from this hour? But that is why I came to this hour" (v. 27).

Troubled? The term (*tarasso*) Jesus used means to be stirred up, agitated, perplexed, even confused. Unknown to those around him, unperceived by those closest to him, Jesus had already begun his suffering. And it got worse as the hours passed.

He asked a question: "What should I say—Father, save Me from this hour?" It was a rhetorical question that assumed no for an answer. Yet, in the dark of a spring night, he would cross through the Kidron Valley, past pilgrims camped there for the holy days, and up the slope of the Mount of Olives, and going into a private garden, he would begin to pray a prayer that included, "Take this cup away from Me" (Mark 14:36a).

Now the crowds were gone. The bustle of Passover was behind him. In the darkness, he traveled a short distance to pray.

The paintings of this event show a serene Jesus in heart-filled prayer, but there is nothing serene about it. Let's look closer at the scene.

If we combine the Matthew and Mark passages, then break the rules of grammar about redundancy, we get an awkward but revealing narration of what Jesus experienced: "Then they came to a place named Gethsemane, and He told His disciples, 'Sit here while I pray.' He took Peter, James, and John with Him, and He was overwhelmed with deep distress, amazement, alarm, and was horrified, heavy, uncomfortable, unfamiliar, and distraught. 'My soul is so surrounded with grief that I am close to dying.'"

The sentence may be cumbersome, but the image is real. Jesus was stricken with crushing emotions. So much so, it weakened him, draining his physical strength. Emotions are powerful things. The very word—*emotion*—means to move within. Think of strong emotions you've felt: the joy of love, the heat of anger, the pain of shock. They're all experienced physically. Often we think of emotions as being mental things—intangible experiences. As true as that is, they have a powerful physical impact. A person's anger can be seen by his red face, tense neck, tight jaw, stare, and body language. An irate person needn't utter a single word for others to know he's angry.

If you've ever been with anyone who received horrible news such as the death of a loved one, you've probably seen the person grab his stomach or bend over. Shocking news or sights have caused people to faint or even to vomit. Emotions are as much a thing of the body as they are of the mind.

Jesus was fully human as well as fully God. We know he ate, felt hunger, slept, and did things other humans do. When his passion began, the emotions were crippling. Mark told us Jesus "fell to the ground" (14:35). Matthew told us Jesus "fell facedown" (26:39a). Luke stated that Jesus "knelt down, and began to pray" (22:41b). But the context and language of Luke suggest that Jesus fell to his knees as if driven to that position by the emotional weight on his shoulders.

If we had been standing there, we would have seen Jesus leave eight of his disciples at the stone enclosure that defined the garden and continue on with Peter, James, and John in tow. We would have heard him instruct the three to beware of temptation and then confess that his grief had surrounded him and was besieging his soul. The emotional tonnage on Jesus would be apparent to us and the weight of it would become obvious when he turned and staggered on a few yards only to tumble to the ground, rise, walk, and crash to the ground again.

There is nothing serene or poetic to see here. Instead, we are forced to witness grueling, unpleasant emotions that crashed upon Jesus with tsunami force.

First Blood

Doctors have long known that emotions affect health. Heart disease, blood pressure, and stomach and bowel disorders can stem from unmanaged negative emotions. In Jesus' case, such physical manifestation reached a new level. Only Luke recorded this detail. It's the kind of thing we would expect from an ancient physician such as Luke.[2] "Being in anguish, He prayed more fervently, and His sweat became like drops of blood falling to the ground" (Luke 22:44).

In describing Jesus' torment, Luke used a word found nowhere else in the New Testament: *agonia.* Looks familiar, doesn't it? We get our word *agony* from it. Originally, the term referred to difficult exercise, used to describe a wrestling match. It came to refer to overpowering emotional struggle.

That emotional wrestling match yielded a shocking physical result, one that some have claimed is impossible. Luke's account was extremely short; but, we will see, the emotional and physical toll of Jesus' prayer was mind-numbing. According to Luke, Jesus' prayer was so intense, so fervent, so deeply felt, that he began to sweat great drops of blood. Luke was very descriptive.

First, he described the flow as sweat and used a term found only in this account. Then he described the perspiration as falling drops of blood. The word for drops—*thromboi*—was used only here. It's an interesting choice of terms. It means a thickening, a clot, or a lump. It's a graphic image. Our English word *thrombosis*—the formation of blood clots—is rooted in this term.

Physicians describe this condition as hematidrosis. It is a rare condition with only a handful of cases reported in the twentieth and twenty-first centuries. A National Institute of Health abstract describes a survey of medical literature in which seventy-six such cases were reported. They concluded that psychogenic causes were at the root of the disorder: "Acute fear and intense mental contemplation were found to be the most frequent inciting causes."[3]

Hematidrosis occurs when emotional strain is so intense the capillaries near the surface of the skin burst and the resulting blood mixes with perspiration, hence the phrase "sweating blood."

While this is the most likely explanation, it is hard to overlook Luke's use of terms, especially *thromboi.* Luke described more than blood sweat. He spoke of drops falling like clots. Could Jesus have experienced more than hematidrosis? Very possible, but the Bible doesn't tell us. Luke described sweat becoming "like drops of blood falling to the ground." We have to acknowledge that Luke could have used picturesque speech to get his idea across, and many have concluded just that. They say Jesus didn't sweat blood, only that his sweat ran like blood. Possible but not likely. Luke was speaking like a doctor. Granted, he could not be compared to a modern physician, but he was trained to look for physical signs and use physical descriptions.

Whatever the actual nature of the trauma, it is clear that it taxed Jesus physically, resulting in an unusual disorder.

If we lump the accounts of Matthew, Mark, and Luke together we get a sense of the unrelenting turmoil Jesus experienced. First, we see the emotional factors that led to the physical results:

1. Jesus humbled himself before his disciples.
2. The disciples' inability to understand what was coming even at this late date in Jesus' ministry.

3. Jesus seeing his disciples quibble over who was going to be of first rank in heaven.
4. The graphic portrayal of his own death in the institution of the Lord's Supper.
5. Announcing Judas's betrayal and watching him turn his back and leave, knowing what the traitor was about to do.
6. Three disciples unable to stay awake while Jesus prayed, leaving Jesus to face agony alone. (Luke indicated an angel ministered to Jesus during this time. Perhaps because the disciples could not.)
7. Jesus' concern that his followers would fall into temptation.
8. Jesus' clear knowledge of the physical torment that awaited him.
9. The weight of sin on him who was sinless.
10. His mission to be the substitute object of judgment to spare us the price of sin.
11. The rejection of his kingdom by his own people.
12. Impending death.

Such psychophysical factors would manifest in horrible torment, just as we see in the Garden of Gethsemane. The Gospels list the following key descriptions:

1. *Deeply distressed* (Mark 14:33; Matt. 26:37). The King James Version uses the phrase "sore amazed" (Mark 14:33). The Greek *ekthambeō* means to toss into terror, to be suddenly and thoroughly alarmed.
2. *Horrified* (Mark 14:33). The word Mark used is *adēmoneo*—to be heavy, shocked, uncomfortable, and out of place.

3. *Sorrow* (Mark 14:34; Matt. 26:38). "My soul is swallowed up in sorrow—to the point of death." Grief enveloped him, surrounded him, swallowed him whole, saturated his consciousness.
4. *Anguish* (Luke 22:44). Undiminished agony carries the idea of wrestling, as in a contest, and great physical exertion.
5. *Fervent prayer* (Luke 22:44). Fervency meaning to be stretched out (*ekenos*). Jesus reached out in prayer and was stretched out in torment.

The Two-Sided Prayer

In the midst of this suffering came Jesus' prayer, a heart-squeezing honest appeal: "My Father! If it is possible, let this cup pass from Me" (Matt. 26:39b).

What a prayer! How relentless must the emotion have been to drive Jesus to the ground and pray that God would remove the cup from him. This was his only prayer that went unanswered.

Well, sort of.

The prayer had two sides. First was the plea to make it stop. Let's be honest. That's what Jesus was requesting. It is the very thing he earlier said he would not pray (John 12:27). If the biblical account ended halfway through that prayer, we would see a Savior looking for a back door to make his escape.

But it didn't end there. Instead, despite the crushing, encircling, life-sapping emotion, Jesus finished the simple prayer with, "Yet not as I will, but as You will" (Matt. 26:39b).

Jesus was enduring a psychological trauma so great he began to sweat blood, yet he concluded his prayer with indescribable bravery.

Obedience overcame terror.

The author of Hebrews wrote about it decades later: "During His earthly life, He offered prayers and appeals, with loud cries and tears, to the One who was able to save Him from death, and He was heard because of His reverence. Though a Son, He learned obedience through what He suffered" (Heb. 5:7–8).

Some of the most profound prayers are short and simple. They originate in the deep recesses of the heart and bubble to the top when life seems out of control. There have been times in my life—and probably every believer's life—when my prayer has been reduced to "God, I don't get it."

During my pastor days, I have heard a thousand appeals made by parents for their children. So frequent were these prayers that a shorthand prayer request evolved. During the prayer time before our midweek Bible studies, parents would raise their hands and utter, "Our children." That was all. No lengthy description of the problem, no laying out of the facts, merely a wounded, concerned heart saying in two words what could not be said in a thousand.

Jesus' prayer bore the brilliant beauty of brevity. Often short prayers pumped out by an aching heart are more eloquent than any poet can pen. Words were inadequate tools to express the need and the emotion. A handful of words did the work.

Resolved to Move Forward

The picture must remain balanced. Jesus did not tumble to the ground as a coward. He was pressed to the ground a hero. A coward would not have been in the garden at all. What Jesus experienced was genuine and enables us to have a Savior to whom we can relate. The pressure, fear, burden, and concern were all real and magnified; but, nonetheless, Jesus remained. He prayed. He sweat drops of blood. But he remained at the place where his arrest would happen.

Courage has never been the absence of fear but the conquest of fear. Seeing Jesus slumped on the dew-covered ground might cause some to view him as a nearly defeated man. Nothing could be further from the truth. There on the ground, Jesus waged war and overcame the human urge to flee so that he might continue the godly desire to finish his ministry. He is the personification of the hero.

Three times Jesus prayed (Matt. 26:44), then something remarkable happened.

He changed.

As though someone flipped a switch, Jesus, who had prayed that the cup of torment be removed from him, rose, approached his disciples and told them the time of his arrest had come. From this moment on, Jesus was in control of all that happened around him. He faced the mob of hundreds who came to arrest him, endured Judas's kiss of betrayal, and healed a slave's ear when Peter lopped it off with a sword.

Viewed through the pages of the Bible, the events that followed showed a Jesus who could not be intimidated by power or the fear of death. He was determined to go to the cross and the tomb and be resurrected. But before he could do those things, he had to spend time in darkness, emotionally squeezed in a garden named Oil Press.

The picture that I, like so many others, have carried with me through the years falls short of the reality. Perhaps our distaste for such garish imagery makes us want to sanitize the Garden of Gethsemane, but doing so does an injustice to Jesus. No painting, image, or description in a book like this can do justice to what the Savior went through.

When he rose from his prayer position on the cold ground, Jesus did so with skin stained by sweat-blood, muscles that surely ached after such profound tension, hair matted by perspiration, and faced the darkness ahead.

Out of that darkness would shine the bright light of the Resurrection.

Chapter 3

The Death Jesus Died

When Mel Gibson released his movie *The Passion of the Christ,* it caused a national stir. Not because it was "religious," but because it was accurate. Some feared a backlash against Jews. Others thought—and this is the amazing part—the violence presented was gratuitous. In a culture in which movies routinely show explosions, murder, rape, dismemberment, and other violent acts, it is difficult to believe that a film about an actual event would receive such nonsensical criticism.

Perhaps that is where the problem lay. Gibson portrayed not fiction but history. Real violence is far more shocking than movie make-believe.

Seeing a man tortured unsettles us, as it should. Torture is a stain that mars history, dating back nearly to the beginning. We often think such cruelty was left behind centuries ago. The rack, iron maiden, and branding were things less civilized people used. But then the news comes on television, and we see mass graves, battered political prisoners, and tortured soldiers.

Presented with such unpleasantness, we avert our attention. I would much rather watch a sitcom than see a video of someone being beaten. Perhaps that is why we so often turn away from the physical torment endured by Christ. This is a book about what Jesus did after his resurrection, but the path to those events first ran through the shadow of the cross. And before there was a cross, there were the dark streets and buildings of Jerusalem.

The Very Physical Jesus

Witnessing the onslaught of emotions experienced by Jesus in the garden reminds us that Jesus, although being God in the flesh, was very human. His emotions led to physical torment. Now, it got worse. In the hands of his captors, Jesus would undergo a series of afflictions difficult to imagine.

The truth that must always be borne in mind is that Jesus had a body. In the context of a book like this, that seems something too obvious to say. Our brains, however, are very good at stripping away the reality of events that happened long ago. How many of us share the feeling of fear of those soldiers who in June of 1944 stormed Normandy, or of the 1970 Apollo 13 astronauts who, after an oxygen tank explosion on their spacecraft, believed their final days would be spent in the cold vacuum of space, their families left earthbound, waiting? For most of us, those are historical events and little more. Those involved, however, knew them to be the life-and-death events they were.

With Jesus' suffering, we must force ourselves to look at the pain, injustice, and sacrifice he endured for us. Only then can we come close to turning history into life-altering truth.

Pre–Crucifixion Brutality

The torture of Christ came in six phases, most with escalating brutality. After his anguished prayer in the Garden of Gethsemane, Jesus rose, gathered his disciples, and moved toward the mob that came to arrest him. *Mob* is the right word. Jesus stood with eleven disciples and possibly Mark, who had come to warn them (Mark 14:51–52).[1] This small band faced a group that included (Matt. 26:47–56; Mark 14:43–52; Luke 22:47–53; John 18:1–11):

1. Judas the traitor.
2. The chief priests (high-ranking priests).
3. Scribes (experts in the Law of Moses and the academics of the day).
4. Elders (administrators).
5. Officers (administrators) of the temple.
6. Pharisees (ultraconservative religious group and perpetual enemies of Jesus).
7. Slaves of the priests and elders.
8. Cohort (a division of a Roman legion that numbered six hundred).

They all showed up to arrest Jesus. The size of the crowd could have easily reached 750 although we have no way of knowing the exact count. It was an overwhelming sight. Add to the fact they brought swords and clubs, and we can begin to imagine the terror the disciples felt.

After Judas's betrayal kiss, Jesus was bound and led away, exchanging the darkness of the garden for the darkness of trials. During those trials, he was subject to physical abuse and emotional mockery.

Phase 1: Before Caiaphas, Annas, and the Sanhedrin

The bound Savior was first taken to the home of Annas, the former high priest (John 18:13). Rome deposed him in AD 15, but his influence remained. Five of his sons and his son-in-law Caiaphas served in the role. Caiaphas was the official high priest during Jesus' trial, but much of the power behind the position lay with Annas.

Here the physical brutality began. Annas pressed Jesus for information about his disciples and his teaching (John 18:19–24), but Jesus refused to cooperate with easy answers. Instead, Christ said, "I have spoken openly to the world . . . . I have always taught in the synagogue and in the temple complex, where all the Jews congregate, and I haven't spoken anything in secret. Why do you question Me? Question those who heard what I told them. Look, they know what I said" (vv. 20–21).

That answer prompted one of the temple police to slap Jesus. The word John used (18:22) means to strike with an open hand. Striking a bound man was not only cruel but cowardly and insulting.

It didn't end with a slap. Luke recorded, "The men who were holding Jesus started mocking and beating Him. After blindfolding Him, they kept asking, 'Prophesy! Who hit You?' And they were saying many other blasphemous things against Him" (22:63–65).

The word (*derovtes*) Luke used for "beating" means to flail or whip. It's not just one man doing the beating. The term is in the plural. Several men were beating Jesus.

When the sport was over, the former high priest sent Jesus to the reigning high priest, Caiaphas. Caiaphas was high priest from AD 27 to 36. As a Sadducee, he had a bone to pick with Jesus. Sadducees were a religious party that accepted only the books of Moses as Scripture, denied the existence of angels, and did not believe in the Resurrection. Jesus quoted from many other Old Testament books and taught about his own resurrection, as well as raising Lazarus and others from the dead.

Caiaphas assembled the Sanhedrin, the religious "supreme court" in Jerusalem. There they grilled Jesus and accused him of crimes against God and Israel. This court met to weigh disputes, but that night it was summoned to pass judgment on an innocent man.

What began in the home of Annas continued in the courtroom of the Sanhedrin, all done in the full view of the high priest. Matthew and Mark painted the ugly picture:

> Then they spit in His face and beat [*kolaphizo*—to strike with the fist] Him; others slapped [*rapizo*—strike with open hand, whip, hit with an instrument] Him and said, "Prophesy to us, Messiah! Who hit [*paio*—sting, strike, smite] You?" (Matt. 26:67–68)
>
> "You have heard the blasphemy! What is your decision?" And they all condemned Him to be deserving of death. Then some began to spit on Him, to blindfold Him, and to beat [*kolaphizo*—

> to strike with the fist] Him, saying, "Prophesy!" Even the temple police took Him and slapped [*rapisma*—strike with open hand] Him. (Mark 14:64–65)

Before the sun had come up, Jesus had already taken a pummeling at the hands of religious leaders and temple guards.

Phase 2: First Appearance before Pilate

Pontius Pilate is one of the best known people in history, not for his leadership skills but for his unwillingness to protect a man he declared innocent. Hated by the Jews he governed, the fifth governor of Judea was handed more than he could handle.

To those who conspired against Jesus, Pilate was a tool and nothing more. Rome did not allow others to execute criminals. Only the Roman government could do that. For Jesus to die, a high-ranking Roman authority would have to permit it. Pilate was the man. Normally, he ruled from the coastal city of Caesarea, but he was in Jerusalem to oversee the crowds who had come for Passover. It was during such crowded times that stresses between the Jews and their conquerors could reach the flash point. They did, but not in the way he expected.

To stand before Pilate was to stand before a man who loathed Jews and had put many to death. In an "urban improvement" project, Pilate wanted to build an aqueduct to Jerusalem from a water source twenty-five miles away. Like all construction projects, it was an expensive proposition. To help fund the effort, the governor used money from the

Jewish temple treasury, money given to support the temple and its religious functions. To the Jews this was intolerable, and they protested in great numbers. Pilate ordered soldiers to surround the gathering, and when that did not quell the protest, he ordered the military to move in. According to the ancient historian Josephus, the armed men attacked and left scores of protestors and bystanders dead.[2] This event may be what Luke 13:1 refers to: "At that time, some people came and reported to Him about the Galileans whose blood Pilate had mixed with their sacrifices."

It is doubtful that Pilate was moved by Jesus' battered appearance. What one Jew did to another was of no concern to him. He tried to dismiss the whole thing, but the accusations brought by the religious leaders were well thought out. They laid out a three-part indictment. They accused Jesus of (1) subverting the Jewish nation, (2) opposing the payment of taxes to Caesar, and (3) claiming to be Messiah the King (Luke 23:2). Any one of those charges could get a man sent to the cross, especially the last one.

But Pilate was not a stupid man. He knew when someone was manipulating him and declared he found "no grounds for charging this man." After learning that Jesus was from Galilee, a district in the north, he passed Jesus off to the man who was charged with that area: Herod Antipas.

This was the only phase of Christ's trial when physical abuse was absent.

Phase 3: Appearance before Herod

Moving from Pilate to Herod Antipas was not a move up. It was Herod who had John the Baptist beheaded. Jesus warned his followers about the tetrarch (Mark 8:15) and called him "that fox" (Luke 13:32; not a compliment in ancient times). Even the Pharisees, early in Jesus' ministry, warned him, "Herod wants to kill You!" (Luke 13:31).

Jesus wouldn't have to travel far since Herod, like most people in the land, was in Jerusalem for Passover, resting in the Herodian Palace. Jesus' keepers walked him through the city, the morning sun climbing high in the sky. Herod pressed for miracles. Before Herod stood a battered man, and Herod's greatest desire was to be entertained (see Luke 23:6–12).

Again, Jesus refused to play along. During this time the ranking priests and scribes stood to the side, shouting accusations about fabricated crimes, egging Herod to do more than merely ask questions. Herod's patience reached an end, and he ordered that Jesus be "treated . . . with contempt" (*exoutheneo*) and "mocked" (*empaizo*).

It was an odd order, and it's unclear exactly what Herod and the others did. To treat with contempt means to reduce the value of Jesus to nothing, to zero him out. To Herod and everyone present, he was to be considered a non-Jew and less than human. Luke revealed an interesting detail: Herod and his soldiers also treated Jesus with contempt. Perhaps that means nothing more than they joined the chief priests, scribes, and others who were there in mocking and accusing Jesus. Or it may mean the soldiers were free to treat Jesus in ways no Jew would treat another.

It is difficult to imagine that this did not involve some physical abuse. It certainly included mental cruelty. They dressed Jesus in a "brilliant robe" and sent him back to Pilate. No doubt the robe was meant to embarrass Jesus, dressing him like a king. How little Herod knew.

This "dress-up" ridicule had an unusual historical impact. "That very day Herod and Pilate became friends. Previously, they had been hostile toward each other" (Luke 23:12). Pilate got the joke and the message. He was free to do with Jesus as he saw fit. This little detail tells us a great deal about Pilate. He was a man who found humor in the suffering of another. Although he was a leader bound by the laws of Roman justice, he was not a man who sympathized with the plight of others, especially a person he assumed Jesus to be.

Despite the moment of entertainment Herod had provided, Pilate was now stuck with a problem he didn't want.

Phase 4: Second Appearance before Pilate

Back through the streets of Jerusalem, the crowded city was now full of life. People moved through the streets, vendors plied their trade, children played, and life continued as if nothing had changed in the previous predawn and early morning hours. People stopped and stared at the man in the bright robe being escorted by temple police past the temple grounds to the four-towered, stone-buttressed walls of the Antonia Fortress, also known as the Praetorium.

Pilate and his soldiers were forced to deal with an issue he thought he had passed off to Herod Antipas. Assessing the mob of accusers and the gathering crowd, Pilate declared Jesus innocent but offered to have him whipped (Luke 23:16). Again, we find something interesting in the original language of the New Testament. Luke used a word (*paideuo*) that means to chastise as a father disciplines a son. It was corporal punishment meant to teach a lesson. Perhaps he meant a lighter beating. It seems Pilate was saying, "OK, I can see this man has gotten under your skin. As a favor to you, I'll have him beaten and that should teach him a lesson."

But Jesus' accusers were not after punishment; they were set on seeing Jesus hang from a cross and made certain Pilate knew it.

The story took a bizarre turn. In the Antonia Fortress was another battered man—Barabbas. All four Gospels mention him by name, describing him as an insurrectionist, a thief, a murderer, and a notorious man. Pilate stood the two men before the gathered crowd and promised to release one. It was his Passover custom, a way of appeasing the people he governed.

It seemed an easy choice. Jesus the rabbi or Barabbas the criminal. But stirred up by the religious leaders, the crowd did something that still baffles people two millennia later: the people called for the release of Barabbas and the crucifixion of Jesus.

There is symbolic irony in this. *Barabbas* means "son of Abba" or "son of the father." In addition, several ancient manuscripts[3] give Barabbas's first name: Jesus. Standing to the right and left of Pilate, respectively, were Jesus Barabbas and Jesus the Christ. Where Barabbas was a son of the father in name, Jesus was (and is) the literal Son of the Father.

Looking deeper, we see further ironies. Barabbas was charged with insurrection, and so was Jesus. Barabbas was guilty; Jesus was innocent. Barabbas sought a political kingdom; Jesus brought a spiritual kingdom.

Barabbas had already been convicted and was sentenced to die on the cross. How poignant that Jesus died on a cross meant for someone else. Barabbas went free because Jesus went to the cross.

Every time I look at this scene, I am reminded that Barabbas represents me. Jesus paid for my crimes so I could be free. I often wonder what Barabbas thought in the days that followed.

As for Jesus, he stood before the very people he had come to save and listened to them call for the release of another man. His rejection was public and complete.

Under pressure from the crowd, perhaps fearing a riot, Pilate let the guilty man walk into the morning sunlight and sent Jesus into the bowels of the Antonia Fortress.

What happened there would turn most men's stomachs.

Phase 5: Military Mistreatment

Earlier, we noted that Pilate offered to have Jesus whipped and saw how the original Greek word used by Luke referred to a beating meant to be instructional. But now things changed. Since the people chose Barabbas, Pilate turned Jesus over to his soldiers and ordered them to scourge him. "Then he released Barabbas to them. But after having Jesus flogged, he handed Him over to be crucified" (Matt. 27:26).

Flogging was a horrible act, and no words can describe the pain inflicted during the process. First, the military men did as ordered and tied Jesus to a post or to metal fasteners in the stone wall of the fortress. Most likely this was done in public with Jerusalem's citizens and visitors watching.

He was stripped, and a soldier took a special whip designed for this one purpose and brought it down on tender skin. The whip used in flogging was called a flagellum and had a wood handle and several long leather straps. Each strap was embedded with something to tear or batter the skin: bits of bone, lead weights, shards of metal. The whip would be brought down on Jesus' shoulders, back, buttocks, and legs. Eusebius described the beating as so severe that "the very inward veins and arteries [were] laid open."[4]

No one knows how long the beating lasted. We assume it all but killed Jesus because we know he was too weak to carry his cross and another man was pressed into service bearing what Jesus could not. However long it was, it left Jesus a tormented, bloody mess. Still he survived, but the abuse wasn't over.

Having completed their assigned task of flogging Jesus, the soldiers were now free to do what they wished before his crucifixion. Matthew 27:27–31 describes it: "Then the governor's soldiers took Jesus into headquarters and gathered the whole company around Him. They stripped Him and dressed Him in a scarlet robe. They twisted together a crown of thorns, put it on His head, and placed a reed in His right hand. And they knelt down before Him and mocked Him: 'Hail, King of the Jews!' Then they spit at Him, took the reed, and kept hitting Him on the head. When they had mocked Him, they stripped Him of the robe, put His clothes on Him, and led Him away to crucify Him."

At some point our imaginations want to shut down. The mind struggles to imagine that men can be so cruel, yet we know they are. This was not punishment for a crime; it was sport. Matthew told us the "whole company" gathered around him. That would be the same six hundred soldiers who helped arrest Jesus. Six hundred men gathered around Jesus and took turns spitting, mocking, and hitting him. When they struck him, they did so with a reed. The word can mean cane, staff, or stalk. Since they had placed the reed in Jesus' hand as though it was a scepter for a king, we can assume it was more than a freshly cut reed. Possibly it was akin to bamboo.

In mind-upending vindictiveness, someone plaited a strand of thorns into a crown and forced it down upon Jesus' head. No one knows which plant was used to make the painful device, nor does it matter. Thorns of any length pressed into the scalp and forehead would be agonizing and humiliating.

While the crown of thorns rested on Jesus' head, the soldiers took turns hitting him on the head with the reed they had given him, adding injury to insult and driving the thorns deeper. Again, we have no idea how long this lasted, but every moment must have been agony for Christ.

Not included in the Gospels is a gruesome detail recorded in an Old Testament prophecy: "I gave My back to those who beat Me, / and My cheeks to those who tore out My beard. / I did not hide My face from scorn and spitting" (Isa. 50:6). Plucking of the beard was painful and, to the Jews of the day, humiliating.

There Jesus stood, slapped multiple times, battered by fists, his back flogged and scalp wounded, beaten over the head with a rodlike reed, and hunks of his beard missing. Heartbreaking to imagine, yet he endured it all. It's no wonder he prayed what he did in the Garden of Gethsemane.

And the cross still lay ahead.

Phase 6: Crucifixion—Six Hours on the Cross

We use the word *excruciating* to describe something extremely painful. The word comes from the Latin and means "out of the cross." The biblical accounts of the Crucifixion are recorded in Matthew 27:32–56; Mark 15:21–41; Luke 23:26–49; and John 19:17–37.

That Jesus could start his journey to Golgotha carrying the heavy crossbeam is remarkable. Still, the agonizing prayer in the garden, the rejections, trials, and beatings took their toll. Matthew, Mark, Luke, and John each tell that a passerby named Simon of Cyrene was pressed into service and bore the heavy wood plank the rest of the way to the spot where Jesus would die.

An entire book can be written about what happened on and near the cross. Our purposes, however, cause us to focus on the physical insult Jesus endured and that led to his death so we might better understand the events following the Resurrection.

Crucifixion was horrible. Even ancient historians shunned the details. So vicious was the torment that Roman law forbade it ever being used on a Roman citizen.

Certain assumptions must be made about the cross because there is much we don't know. Arguments have been waged over the shape of the cross. Jesus is often portrayed dragging the full cross along a Jerusalem street, although he probably carried only the cross member. Either way, it was grueling.

Once at the crucifixion site, the guards assigned to Jesus would have stripped him naked. His clothing—headwear, sandals, outer garment (cloak), inner garment (tunic), and girdle—was divided among the four soldiers (John 19:23). The inner garment was seamless and therefore very valuable. They cast lots for the tunic rather than tear it and by doing so fulfilled a prophesy in Psalm 22:18.

The already battered and exhausted Jesus, still in pain from his beatings, was laid on the crossbeam. In some cases, the soldiers would pull the victim's arms and legs out of joint to inflict greater pain and to keep the condemned helpless. Square iron nails were pounded through Jesus' hands.

Some have argued that the nails must have been placed to pierce the wrist because the muscles, tendons, and bones of the hand were too weak to have held Jesus to the cross. However, each time Jesus showed his wounds after the Resurrection, the Greek word used is *cheir,* the common term for hand. In some cases, to prolong the agony, Romans crucified their victims without nails, merely tying them to the cross and leaving them there for days on end. Most likely, Jesus' arms were tied to the crossbeam and his hands punctured with the rough nails.

Next, the crossbeam would be raised up the vertical member of the cross and set on a large pin. If the whole cross rested on the ground, which is also possible, then the cross and man would be raised and the base of the crucifix dropped into a hole.

The tormentors would then have crossed Jesus' feet and driven a spike through them, very probably through a piece of wood first. It is possible that Jesus was nailed through the ankles, one nail through each ankle as his feet straddled the upright post. In 1968, an archaeologist discovered a pierced ankle bone of a young man named John. It appears he was a victim of crucifixion, and his feet were nailed to the post through the side. This doesn't mean that every crucifixion happened this way, only that some did.

When the Romans wanted to stretch out the torment, a board would be placed beneath the condemned's buttocks so he could rest some of his weight. It is doubtful that such was done in Jesus' case. Because of the pending Sabbath and to avoid creating new problems with the Jews, Pilate and the others were looking for a quick death. To speed the arrival of death, they broke the legs of the two criminals crucified with Jesus. When they came to Christ, they found he had already died (John 19:33).

The crucified died for several reasons: shock, unremitting pain, and suffocation as his strength waned and he was no longer able to straighten enough to breathe. It's a humbling thought to know that each time Jesus spoke from the cross, he had to press down against the spike through his feet to be able to draw enough air to utter words.

Six hours is a long time to live on a cross, especially after all Jesus had endured. Considering the rejection, mocking, and the crushing weight of bearing humanity's sin, we wonder how Jesus lasted that long.

Still, even hanging from the cross, he had work to do. He had a sermon to preach, but the very nature of crucifixion prohibited lengthy conversation. Instead, like a preacher behind a pulpit, Jesus referred to his text, *"'Elí, Elí, lemá sabachthâni?'* that is, 'My God, My God, why have You forsaken Me?'" (Matt. 27:46). In Jesus' day, not having Bibles with chapters and verses as we do today, teachers referred to biblical passages by citing the first or dominant verse. In a loud voice, Jesus drew the attention of every Jew within hearing to Psalm 22. He was not making a plea; he was quoting Scripture.

Psalm 22 is a depiction of crucifixion a thousand years before it happened, and not just any crucifixion. The details show that the ancient text refers to Jesus' specific situation, including the casting of lots for his garments. Those standing by would make the connection.

Psalm 22 is profound on many counts, but it is especially significant because it emphasizes the physical torment Jesus would endure nearly ten centuries later. The psalmist foresaw:

- Weakness: "I am poured out like water" (v. 14).
- Dislocation of the joints: "All my bones are disjointed" (v. 14).
- Incapacitation: "My heart is like wax, melting within me" (v. 14).
- Exhaustion: "My strength is dried up like baked clay" (v. 15).
- Dehydration: "My tongue sticks to the roof of my mouth" (v. 15).
- Impalement: "They pierced my hands and my feet" (v. 16).
- Hyperextension: "I can count all my bones" (v. 17).

Also during those hours, Jesus passed the care of his mother to one of his disciples (John 19:26–27) and promised salvation to one of the repentant crucified thieves (Luke 23:43). All this he did while engulfed in the most intense agony.

At about three that afternoon, Jesus took what breath he could and cried out, "Father, into Your hands I entrust My spirit" (Luke 23:46). Then he breathed his last.

Crucifixion was meant to be a slow, torturous death. Jesus died before anyone expected him to. When Joseph of Arimathea asked Pilate for permission to have the body, the governor was surprised to hear that Jesus was already dead (Mark 15:44). Jesus had done what he came to do and willingly gave up his spirit.

The final insult to Jesus' body came at the hands of one of the soldiers who had crucified him. "But one of the soldiers pierced His side with a spear, and at once blood and water came out" (John 19:34). We can't know for certain why water and blood, but several good possibilities exist. One is that the soldier pressed the spearpoint through the skin and lung and nicked the heart. The blood would come from the wound to skin, muscle, and organs, and the water from stress-induced fluids accumulated between the heart and the pericardium.

The spike through the feet was jerked free, and Jesus' body was taken down from the cross, a battered mess of human tissue. The nails were pulled from the hands and the wood beneath. Jesus lay on the dirt, pummeled, abused, and now dead. It breaks the heart to think that Mary his mother saw all this, as did John and others.

The image is humbling. This Jesus did for me and for you. Earlier we spoke of the accurate prophesy and emphasis on the physical side of the torment in Psalm 22. Isaiah 53 does a similar thing but makes it more personal:

> Who has believed what we have heard? And who has the arm of the LORD been revealed to? He grew up before Him like a young plant and like a root out of dry ground. He had no form or splendor that we should look at Him, no appearance that we should desire Him. He was despised and rejected by men, a man of suffering who knew what sickness was. He was like one people turned away from; He was despised, and we didn't value Him.

Yet He Himself bore our sicknesses, and He carried our pains; but we in turn regarded Him stricken, struck down by God, and afflicted. But He was pierced because of our transgressions, crushed because of our iniquities; punishment for our peace was on Him, and we are healed by His wounds. We all went astray like sheep; we all have turned to our own way; and the Lord has punished Him for the iniquity of us all.

He was oppressed and afflicted, yet He did not open His mouth. Like a lamb led to the slaughter and like a sheep silent before her shearers, He did not open His mouth. He was taken away because of oppression and judgment; and who considered His fate? For He was cut off from the land of the living; He was struck because of My people's rebellion. They made His grave with the wicked, and with a rich man at His death, although He had done no violence and had not spoken deceitfully.

Yet the Lord was pleased to crush Him, and He made Him sick. When You make Him a restitution offering, He will see [His] seed, He will prolong His days, and the will of the Lord will succeed by His hand. He will see [it] out of His anguish, and He will be satisfied with His knowledge. My righteous servant will justify many, and He will carry their iniquities. Therefore I will give Him the many as a portion, and He will receive the mighty as spoil, because He submitted Himself to death, and was counted among the

> rebels; yet He bore the sin of many and interceded for the rebels.

Jesus told of the beatings he would endure and spoke of his cross. He knew it was coming, and he knew the details. Luke recorded a couple of instances when Jesus let it be known what the future held for him.

> But He strictly warned and instructed them to tell this to no one, saying, "The Son of Man must suffer many things and be rejected by the elders, chief priests, and scribes, be killed, and be raised the third day." (9:21–22)
>
> Then He took the Twelve aside and told them, "Listen! We are going up to Jerusalem. Everything that is written through the prophets about the Son of Man will be accomplished. For He will be handed over to the Gentiles, and He will be mocked, insulted, spit on; and after they flog Him, they will kill Him, and He will rise on the third day." (18:31–33)

Still he went. And for that, no words can express the necessary gratitude.

Chapter 4

From Wood Cross to Stone Tomb

One of Jesus' most gripping miracles happened outside a tomb just two miles from Jerusalem. The village of Bethany was home to three of Jesus' closest friends and supporters: Mary, Martha, and Lazarus. It was one of the Savior's frequent stops. John 11 tells of a special journey Jesus made to the town. Days before he had received word that Lazarus had died. One would think that Jesus would immediately have left to join the funeral procession, at very least. Instead, he lingered and didn't arrive on the scene until four days later.

The event that followed helps us understand what happened to Jesus after his death on the cross and before his resurrection. Those familiar with the story know that Jesus raised Lazarus back to life (see John 11:1–44). By New Testament standards, it's a rather long story, but for our purposes we want to freeze the frame on only a few moments.

Jesus stood before a tomb, most likely one that had been hewed out of a limestone hill as many such burial chambers were. A large stone sealed the opening. The moment Jesus commanded the stone be removed, he was told Lazarus had been inside for four days and he would "stink" (John 11:39). It's a clue about how first-century Jews buried their dead.

Fearful odors not withstanding, Jesus insisted the stone be removed. Jesus prayed, then shouted, "Lazarus, come out!" (v. 43).

Lazarus did, "bound hand and foot with linen strips and with his face wrapped in a cloth" (v. 44). Hit the pause button. In that moment, Jesus was facing a man who had been prepared for burial the same way he would be later.

To understand the behavior of those who witnessed the resurrection appearances of Christ, and having seen the physical damage done from the Garden of Gethsemane through the trials and ultimately on the cross, we must also see what was done to the body of Jesus immediately following the Crucifixion.

How to Bury a First-Century Man

Burial customs vary according to culture. In the Western world, we let professionals take care of matters. If a friend or family member dies in a hospital, we might not see the body again until the funeral, and then only if there is an open casket. If someone dies at home, at least in the United States, the body is removed and subject to autopsy unless the person was under a physician's care and death was expected. Again, the body isn't seen until the funeral.

In Jesus' day things were very different—especially for the Jews. When a person died, things moved quickly. Usually the person was buried the same day, an important fact in a world without embalming or refrigeration.

It was the obligation of family and sometimes close friends to care for the body. Two men stepped forward to take on the task. The first was Joseph of Arimathea. He is mentioned in all four of the Gospels (Matt. 27:57–66; Mark 15:42–47; Luke 23:50–56; John 19:38–42). He was described as a "disciple" (Matt. 27:57), "a prominent member of the Sanhedrin" (Mark 15:43), "a good and righteous man . . . who had not agreed with [the Sanhedrin's] plan and action" (Luke 23:50–51), and a secret follower (John 19:38).

The death of Jesus propelled Joseph out of the shadows and into public scrutiny as a follower of Christ. While others had called for Christ's death, Joseph assumed responsibility for the body of Jesus.

He was not alone. Nicodemus stood shoulder to shoulder with Joseph. Only John recorded this fact. Indeed, John was the only writer to record anything done by the religious leader. It was Nicodemus who came to Jesus under the cover of night to ask questions and to whom Jesus taught the principle of new birth (John 3:1–21). He appeared again in John, defending Jesus before the chief priests and Pharisees and receiving a snide remark for his trouble (7:45–52). Last, we see him ministering to the body of Jesus, taking seventy-five pounds[1] or so of myrrh and aloes (John 19:39–40).

Only two men of all those who had followed. Stepping forward was not only brave but important to God's plan. If no one claimed the body of Jesus, it would have been carried to the Hinnom Valley outside the southern wall of Jerusalem and dropped into the smoldering community dump.

At this point we might wonder where Jesus' earthly family was. We know Mary his mother was at the cross, but what of his brothers and sisters? Matthew 13:55–56 mentions four brothers: James, Joseph, Simon, and Judas, as well as unnamed and unnumbered sisters. Where were they during the Crucifixion, and why did they not assume the family's responsibility to care for and bury the body? We are not told, but it is safe to assume they were many miles to the north in their home region of Galilee. It's likely that Mary the mother of Jesus often traveled with Jesus. Perhaps the family had traveled to Jerusalem for Passover and left early. Maybe they hadn't come at all.

It appears that Mary had no other family with her.[2] Perhaps that was why Jesus looked to John to care for his mother (John 19:27). Tradition holds that John took care of Mary for the remainder of her days.

In the absence of family, who could carry out the burial duties? With the sun setting, Joseph of Arimathea and Nicodemus assumed the responsibility. The corpse would be washed and sometimes anointed with perfume. Mary (not the mother of Jesus) poured perfume on Jesus while he was alive and received harsh criticism for doing so, but Jesus defended her saying, "Leave her alone; she has kept it for the day of My burial. For you always have the poor with you, but you do not always have Me" (John 12:7–8).

After the body was cleaned, the arms would be folded over the front and the wrists tied with a strip of linen. A band of cloth would also be wrapped around the head and under the jaw to keep the mouth shut. Linen strips would then be wrapped around the body from the feet to under the arms. The linen was applied with myrrh and aloe between the overlapping layers.

After the torso was wrapped with the cloth strips and the perfume, myrrh, and aloes applied, a face napkin—a square of cloth—was laid over the face of Jesus. The body was then moved to the grave. We get insight into how this was done from a miracle performed by Jesus many months before.

In the small community of Nain southwest of the Sea of Galilee, Jesus and his band encountered a funeral (Luke 7:11–17). A young man, the only son of a widow, had died and was being carried to his burial spot. Jesus was moved with compassion over the woman's plight and after a few words, raised the son back to life. What is important here is the line: "Then He came up and touched the open coffin, and the pallbearers stopped" (v. 14a).

The "open coffin" was probably a bier, a wood stretcher used by pallbearers to convey the young man's body to its burial place. Joseph and Nicodemus may have used a similar device.

Jesus was then buried in a tomb. Ancient Romans cremated their dead, but Jews almost always interred their lost loved ones. When possible, a tomb was used. A tomb might be made from a natural cave or hewed out of a hillside. The rich, like Joseph, could afford custom-made tombs.

Tombs were designed to be reused with one family member being buried after another as the need arose. The body was left to—for lack of a more polite term—decay. Since Jews did not embalm or mummify, the body would deteriorate quickly. When just the skeleton remained, the tomb would be opened, the bones collected and placed in a box, often made of limestone, called an ossuary. The name of the dead might be engraved on the container.

Inside the tomb would be a rock or wood bench on which the body would be laid. Family members would pay their final respects, leave, and seal the tomb's entrance with a large stone. The stone was often round so it could be rolled into place or rolled away when the tomb was needed again. The purpose of the stone was to keep animals out and the smell of decay in.

The two men who prepared Jesus' body for burial were heroes in their own right. Their work was sacrificial. As Edwin A. Blum said, "Joseph and Nicodemus' act of love and respect for the body of Jesus was for them dangerous, costly, and without any personal gain. The service of Christians for their living Lord should be equally courageous and sacrificial, for their labor is not in vain."[3]

The Stone Rolled Shut

If we were standing there that day two millennia ago, gazing into the tomb, we would have seen Jesus resting on a stone bed—his feet, hands, and jaw tied with linen strips and his legs and torso wrapped with linen treated with aloes, myrrh, and perfume. Since the tomb was new, his was the only corpse present. Joseph and Nicodemus, perhaps aided by servants, closed the stone over the opening, sealing Jesus in and everyone else out.

That circular stone became even more significant because of what happened to it soon after Jesus' burial.

> The next day, which followed the preparation day, the chief priests and the Pharisees gathered before Pilate and said, "Sir, we remember that while this deceiver was still alive, He said, 'After three days I will rise again.' Therefore give orders that the tomb be made secure until the third day. Otherwise, His disciples may come, steal Him, and tell the people, 'He has been raised from the dead.' Then the last deception will be worse than the first."
>
> "You have a guard [of soldiers]," Pilate told them. "Go and make it as secure as you know how." Then they went and made the tomb secure by sealing the stone and setting the guard. (Matt. 27:62–66)

The problem with being part of a conspiracy is it makes one paranoid about other conspiracies. The chief priests and Pharisees were no different. To thwart anyone from stealing the body and claiming Christ's resurrection, they approached Pilate for help. Guards were provided and the stone door sealed.

The seal is a mystery. We don't know how the seal was applied. We assume it refers to the Roman wax seal of Pilate. To break the seal was to ask for punishment and possibly death. A wax patch may have been affixed to the sides of the tomb on either side of the round stone and a cord run between them crossing in front of the stone. Into the wax would be pressed the governor's official seal warning everyone to leave the tomb alone.

Another approach was to place several wax seals around the joint where the exterior tomb wall met the stone door. Moving the stone was impossible without breaking the seals.

In any case, we know the door was sealed with official approval, and guards were posted nearby.

An Interesting Connection

Tradition and many scholars think Mary gave birth to Jesus while secluded in a cave. Animals were often sheltered in caves that served as natural barns. If this was so, the connections between Jesus' birth and burial are as remarkable as they are poetic.

Luke recorded the birth and the angelic announcement:

> In the same region, shepherds were staying out in the fields and keeping watch at night over their flock. Then an angel of the Lord stood before them, and the glory of the Lord shone around them, and they were terrified. But the angel said to them, "Don't be afraid, for look, I proclaim to you good news of great joy that will be for all the people: today a Savior, who is Messiah the Lord, was born for you in the city of David. This will be the sign for you: you will find a baby wrapped snugly in cloth and lying in a manger." (2:8–12)

The last line is heard every Christmas season, often without realizing the portent of the message. Each December we see scores of nativity scenes. These small representations usually have miniatures of Mary, Joseph, a lean-to-like structure, various animals, the three wise men (who didn't arrive until months later), and, of course, baby Jesus resting on a straw-filled, wood feeding trough. These are so familiar to us we seldom question their accuracy. Most of these settings are cute . . . and probably wrong.

The manger was most likely a stone feeding trough or even a stone projection from the cave wall. Such stone feeders were not unusual for the day. They endured the rough jostling of animals and were not prone to damage by insects.

It is also interesting to note that Luke mentioned the baby Jesus being "wrapped snugly in cloth and lying in a manger." In fact, the angelic message was that those two elements were to be "the sign" for the shepherds. The cloth wrappings and stone manger were the identifying marks to be used by the shepherds in recognizing Jesus and the truth of the angelic statement.

Looking at the burial of Christ, we see (and shall see) these connections are more than coincidence. The following chart shows some of the curious ties between the birth and burial of Jesus:

	Birth	**Death**
Location:	Cave	Tomb
Wrapping:	Cloth/swaddling clothes	Linen strips, face napkin, possible shroud
Resting Place:	Stone feeding trough or ledge for animals	Stone ledge in tomb
Ownership:	Borrowed cave	Borrowed tomb
Angels	Announce birth	Announce resurrection
	Joseph (the husband of Mary) present at birth	Joseph of Arimathea present at death

Even in birth, the death of Jesus is seen. From womb to tomb, the purpose of Christ has always been to die for the sins of those he loves.

Chapter 5

The Enigmatic Tomb

When the large stone was rolled into place, sealing Jesus in and everyone else out, it must have seemed the end of the story. Dead is dead and not much can be done about it. Yet, Jesus taught his followers that he would be killed and rise on the third day.[1] As we saw, the teaching was well known enough that the chief priests and Pharisees felt compelled to ask for the tomb to be sealed and guarded. Still, when the time came and the battered body was removed from the cross, his followers must have thought the glorious mission was over.

Then Sunday morning happened. In the pages ahead, we will look at each appearance of Christ and what his words and actions taught; but first we must see one more thing, something often overlooked.

There is no doubt the Resurrection is the linchpin of Christianity. It affects the faithful as a whole but still aims at the heart of the individual. The very fact Christ rose from the dead is so stunning that the details are often eclipsed by the event. It is often said the devil is in the details. That's nonsense. The devil is in the generalities—God is in the details.

When we picture Christ stepping from the tomb, it is almost impossible to see anything else. The event is so grand it blinds us to anything else. Still, those details are what make the Resurrection even more powerful.

No human eyes witnessed the Resurrection event. There were many eyewitnesses to the resurrected Jesus, but no one was in the sealed tomb to see the actual event. There were, however, eyewitnesses of a different kind and clues left behind for us to ponder.

The Resurrection is recorded in each of the four Gospels. Like four painters working on the same canvas, each writer was inspired to record different details. This isn't the result of poor reporting; it is the outcome of intricate planning by God. Each author wrote under the guidance of the Holy Spirit, leaving us who follow a tapestry of truth and facts.

Outside of one or two nonbiblical references from the time, the Bible is the only source (certainly the only dependable source) for the events that happened that early spring day. By weaving together the accounts in the Gospel narratives, we see some unusual things occurred in those first few hours.

Crucial Evidence

The first one to the scene was Mary Magdalene. (We will learn more about Mary in the next chapter.) The sun had crested the horizon and was beginning its slow rise through the sky when Mary, unable to wait any longer, shuffled along the dirt path that led to the garden and the tomb. "Now Mary Magdalene and Mary the mother of Joses were watching where He was placed" (Mark 15:47).

She knew where to go.

She knew where she wanted to be—where she needed to be.

We can only guess what her thoughts were, but we can be certain they were fixed on Jesus and her commitment to him. Through tear-flooded eyes, she got her first shock.

The grave stood open. The stone had been rolled away, the wax seals bearing Pilate's insignia fractured. John 20 gives the details:

> On the first day of the week Mary Magdalene came to the tomb early, while it was still dark. She saw that the stone had been removed from the tomb. So she ran to Simon Peter and to the other disciple, the one Jesus loved, and said to them, "They have taken the Lord out of the tomb, and we don't know where they have put Him!"
>
> At that, Peter and the other disciple went out, heading for the tomb. The two were running together, but the other disciple outran Peter and got to the tomb first. Stooping down, he saw the linen cloths lying there, yet he did not go in. Then, following him, Simon Peter came also. He entered the tomb and saw the linen cloths lying there. The wrapping that had been on His head was not lying with the linen cloths but was folded up in a separate place by itself. The other disciple, who

> had reached the tomb first, then entered the tomb, saw, and believed. For they still did not understand the Scripture that He must rise from the dead. Then the disciples went home again. (vv. 1–10)

In a panic, Mary raced to where Peter was staying. The "other disciple, the one Jesus loved" was John. Breathless from the sprint and from shock, she told them, "They have taken the Lord out of the tomb, and we don't know where they have put Him!"

Peter traced Mary's steps back to the tomb. John was with him every step of the way. As they closed the distance to the garden tomb, John raced ahead, not waiting for Peter. The emotion in these men propelled them forward. John stopped just outside the tomb, perhaps approaching the opening. To touch the dead or anything associated with a corpse would have rendered John ceremonially unclean.[2] Stopping outside the tomb was natural, the result of years of Jewish upbringing. And, to be honest, how many of us would plow into a tomb with a freshly buried body?

Peter was a different story. Mary Magdalene had said Jesus was missing, his body stolen. The truth of that statement could only be verified in the tomb. Peter may have been second to arrive, but he was first inside.

Both men saw the unexpected. John gave provocative details: "Then, following him, Simon Peter came also. He entered the tomb and saw the linen cloths lying there. The wrapping that had been on His head was not lying with the linen cloths but was folded up in a separate place by itself" (20:6–7).

Remember, Joseph of Arimathea and Nicodemus had tied Jesus' hands and wrapped his legs and torso in strips of cloth impregnated with aloes and myrrh. If we were standing there as detectives, we would wonder how Jesus worked himself free from his bonds.

Something else is interesting about this account. New Testament Greek, the language John wrote in, is a detail-oriented tongue. In the English translation for this passage the word saw appears three times. In the original Greek, three different words are used.

The first term means to look, to perceive, to see (from *blepo*). It's the everyday term for *see.* John arrived at the tomb, stooped, and "looked" in.

Next Peter bolted into the sepulcher and *saw* the linens, but the word here (from *theoreo*) means to gaze with interested intent. Peter was looking for clues, trying to make sense of what he was seeing. Peter was puzzled. Something about the linens seized his attention. What was he seeing?

John entered the tomb and saw the same things. He saw (this time from *eidon*) the linens, but the word carries the idea of seeing with understanding, not just a gaze, more than a puzzled stare, but seeing with insight. John "saw and believed." What he saw was convincing. No conversation between the two men is mentioned. No debate. Peter wondered; John saw and believed.

What they saw and studied was the bewildering arrangement of the linens. To one side was the face napkin and perhaps the head tie used to keep the jaw from sagging. They lay on the stone bier, not in a heap, as we would expect if someone were stealing the body, but folded neatly and set to the side. A thief stealing the body of Christ wouldn't bother removing any of the linens. The folding showed deliberation, forethought, and the ease of time.

The other wrappings heighten the enigma. The passage implies the linen wrappings were in the same position they would have been if the body were still there. Instead of a pile of wrappings, they saw a chrysalis, a cocoon, as if Jesus had passed through them without disturbing their position or form. It is possible that the aloe and myrrh mixture spread on and between the linen strips allowed the wrappings to hold their form. No man could wriggle out of such restraints, especially one who had been battered, beaten, flogged, nailed to a cross, and stabbed in the side so deeply the heart was nicked or punctured.

Perhaps their minds ran back to Lazarus as he came out of his tomb, still bound. Lazarus was brought back to life but not in the same way as Jesus. Jesus rose unbound by linen ties or stone door.

No, what happened here, the disciples knew, was far from ordinary. Yet, the passage reveals "they still did not understand the Scripture that He must rise from the dead" (v. 9).

There was nothing to do but go home and wait.

A Pair of Angels

An even more weary Mary Magdalene returned to the tomb. Her sprint to find Peter and the emotional shock of seeing the open tomb had taken its toll. Although it doesn't seem possible, her heart was broken all the more. We don't know if she encountered Peter and John as they returned home. Perhaps so. And even if she had, what would they have told her? "We arrived, we went in and saw where the body had been. The place was empty. Nothing makes sense."

Mary moved to the tomb. She stooped and gazed inside and was surprised to see the tomb no longer empty. "But Mary stood outside facing the tomb, crying. As she was crying, she stooped to look into the tomb. She saw two angels in white sitting there, one at the head and one at the feet, where Jesus' body had been lying" (John 20:11–12).

This was an amazing development. When Mary first arrived, she saw no angels. Peter and John didn't see angels. Why now? Why the "late" arrival? More questions arise when we look at the details. Why does the text tell us the number of angels and that they were sitting where the body of Jesus had been?

Details matter, and seldom does the Bible give a detail without a reason for it. So what is the reason here? A closer look tells us.

A pair of angels sat on the stone bier, one on each end. Resting between them were the grave wrappings that had encompassed Jesus. The image is gripping and the symbolism amazing.

The word *angel* is a generic term. In both the Old and New Testaments the term refers to a messenger, human or otherwise. In the New Testament the term is almost exclusively reserved for that special class of nonhuman beings who serve God. Often angels brought a message from God or carried out his will by some other means. Such is the case here. These angels have a point to make. One they make with words, the other through symbolism.

First the words. "They said to her, 'Woman, why are you crying?'" (John 20:13). At first, the question seems outlandish.

She was weeping because she saw her Savior, beaten, crucified, buried, and now—best as she could tell—someone has pried open his tomb and made off with his body. If anyone had a right to weep, it was Mary Magdalene.

But is that what the angels are asking? Were they puzzled by human emotion? Doubtful. They had seen Jesus weep. Certainly they had viewed the Crucifixion and all those around it. There was weeping there.

The question isn't why there was such an outpouring of emotion, but why did the weeping continue? The question might be translated, "Why do you continue to weep?"

Her answer was from the heart: "Because they've taken away my Lord, and I don't know where they've put Him" (John 20:13b). It was one more indignity piled upon countless other indignities. It was bad enough that Jesus was killed the way he was. To have his grave defiled was more than she could take. Words fall short in trying to describe what Mary must have felt.

A moment later, the angel's point was made clear to Mary. She turned and saw Jesus, becoming the first human to witness the resurrected Jesus. We will see how that played out in the next chapter. For now, let's look back in the tomb.

The angel's unspoken message is often overlooked. What Mary saw was two angels sitting at opposite ends of the funeral bench. Between them rested the blood-stained wrappings. There are several intriguing points about this image.

First, nowhere else are angels described as sitting. We will see four angels are described as sitting at or in the tomb. The question is: Was this significant? Why sit on the funeral bier? Why sit on the ends? This would strike most people as rude.

The fact these details are given tells us something special is going on.

The angels were painting a picture that has remained vivid through the centuries. They were portraying something that came to be fourteen hundred years before.

Moses received a command from God to build a special device. It was a box called an ark. God gave specific dimensions and verbal instructions on how the ark was to be built and what it was to look like. The word *ark* simply means box. The Hebrew term from which it is derived is *anon* and referred to a chest or a coffin. This special chest was called by many names but was best known as the ark of the covenant.

The ark of the covenant was a wood box, covered inside and out with gold plating. It's dimensions were given in cubits. A cubit is a measure of length taken from the end of a man's elbow to the tip of his extended fingers. Since forearm length varies from man to man, a cubit could range from sixteen to twenty-two inches. An average cubit was eighteen inches. If we assume that length, the ark of the covenant would measure about 3.75 feet by 2.25 feet, by 2.25 feet.

God commissioned two men to build the ark: Bezalel and Oholiab. They were gifted artisans who put their talents to work (Exod. 35:30–35). They used only two building materials: gold and wood.

The wood was taken from the acacia tree, a hard-grained, dark, insect-resistant material. Sometimes this wood is called *shittim.* From this material, Bezalel and Oholiab constructed the basic box that formed the ark.

They then plated the hardwood with gold. The entire box was covered with the precious metal so that no wood was showing. The Bible doesn't tell us how thick the gold was. It was certainly more than gold foil but not so thick as to make the ark too heavy to carry long distances. Everything related to the ark was covered in gold, including the carrying poles.

It must have been dazzling to see—except no one was allowed to see it. Only the high priest ever viewed the box. During Moses' day when the ark was moved, it was always covered, hidden from the eyes of common people (Num. 4:5–6).

The ark was capped with a lid—a lid with special significance. The Bible refers to it as the "mercy seat" (*kapporeth*) (Exod. 25:17). The artisans crafted the top from a continuous layer of gold and sculpted a pair of cherubim statues—winged angels whose presence is always associated with the throne of God. The angels were crafted so their faces forever faced the mercy seat and their wings stretched up and forward, touching over the middle of the ark.

Each year on the Day of Atonement, and only on that day, the high priest would enter the most holy place (the Holy of Holies) in the tabernacle (and later the temple) to represent his people before God. Before he could enter, he would make a blood sacrifice for his own sin. After sacrificing a bull, he entered the Holy of Holies and sprinkled blood on the mercy seat. When he entered the room, he wore a linen robe.

The parallels are stunning. What Mary saw was a symbolic representation of what the high priest saw only once a year. Instead of seeing a gold-clad box with two angels kneeling on the lid, Mary saw two angels sitting on the spot where the slain body of Christ had lain, his still blood-stained linen wrappings in place.

In Jesus' day, the ark of the covenant was gone. The high priest would enter the Holy of Holies of the temple and sprinkle blood where the ark and the mercy seat used to be.

Looking through the eyes of Mary, we see a pair of angels sitting on the funeral couch in a similar way the two cherubim sat on the ark of the covenant. The sprinkling of blood was represented by the blood-marred linen stripes. Jesus, as our high priest, sacrificed himself for our sins. Instead of sprinkling the blood of a bull, he shed his own blood. As the ancient high priest would don linen garments before going into the Holy of Holies, Jesus "wore" linen burial wrappings.

Inside the ark of the covenant rested several unique and holy items: the Ten Commandments, a golden jar of manna, and the rod of Aaron. Each of these are symbols of Christ. Jesus was and is the fulfillment of the law (Matt. 5:17). The golden jar of miraculous food called manna was literally bread from heaven. Jesus said of himself, "I am the living bread that came down from heaven. If anyone eats of this bread he will live forever. The bread that I will give for the life of the world is My flesh" (John 6:51).

Also in the ark of the covenant was the rod of Aaron, which, although merely a dead staff, budded to life showing God's choice of him as high priest. A dead piece of wood came back to life and produced buds; what better example of the Resurrection is there?

The author of Hebrews wrote:

> Now the Messiah has appeared, high priest of the good things that have come. In the greater and more perfect tabernacle not made with hands (that is, not of this creation), He entered the holy of holies once for all, not by the blood of goats and calves, but by His own blood, having obtained eternal redemption. For if the blood of goats and bulls and the ashes of a heifer sprinkling those who are defiled, sanctify for the purification of the flesh, how much more will the blood of the Messiah, who through the eternal Spirit offered Himself without blemish to God, cleanse our consciences from dead works to serve the living God? (9:11–14)

The image before Mary would force her mind to the image of the ark of the covenant: a pair of angels, the stone mercy seat, the linen, all a quiet, symbolic revelation about what Christ achieved for humanity. Forgiveness came because of his sacrifice. "According to the law almost everything is purified with blood, and without the shedding of blood there is no forgiveness" (Heb. 9:22).

And this was just the beginning.

The Number Grew

Looking to the other Gospels, we see a bigger picture begins to appear. Mark wrote, "When they entered the tomb, they saw a young man dressed in a long white robe sitting on the right side; they were amazed and alarmed" (16:5). The "they" he spoke of were Mary Magdalene, Mary the mother of James, and Salome (16:1).

As we will see, Mary Magdalene was joined by other women. They had come to the tomb to anoint Jesus' body with more spices, perhaps feeling that the burial preparations had not been enough. They entered the tomb and saw a young man in a white robe seated to the right. This angel shouldn't be confused with the two who sat on the bier, or the one we will see later sitting on the tomb's sealing stone.

The first thing to catch our attention is Mark's use of "young man" (*neaniskos*). He didn't call the individual an angel. The singular word is never used in Mark, but he did use the plural "angels" five times, so the word was part of his writing vocabulary. Why then did he use "young man"? Surely, this person was an angel. He wore the same white robe as the two seated on the bier.

Like two angels seen by Mary, this one was also seated. Why give us that detail? Why not standing, pacing, or leaning against the tomb wall?

In many cultures, sitting represents the end of work, the finishing of a task. But what was this young man's task? If the two angels sitting on the bier represented the two angels on the mercy seat of the ark of the covenant, we are safe in assuming the young man also represented something or someone.

The seated angel typified the high priest who offered sacrifices for the nation of Israel. But with Christ's death, Christ became the high priest who offered the only sacrifice that could forever remove sin. The author of Hebrews said it this way, "Now every priest stands day after day ministering and offering time after time the same sacrifices, which can never take away sins. But this man, after offering one sacrifice for sins forever, sat down at the right hand of God" (10:11–12).

Note that the priests "stand day after day ministering and offering time after time." Then the author stated that Jesus did the work once and for all and forever. There is no longer a need for a priest to make offerings for our sins. Christ's work on the cross did everything that needed to be done. With no more need for blood sacrifices, priests are unneeded. The third seated angel represented the finished work of the high priest.

So far, we have seen three angels, but the tomb was about to become a little more crowded. Luke added two more: "While they were perplexed about this, suddenly two men stood by them in dazzling clothes. So the women were terrified and bowed down to the ground" (24:4–5).

Like Mark, Luke chose not to use the word *angel,* instead describing these two as "men" (*aner*). Unlike the angels we've seen so far, their clothing was "dazzling," flashing, sparkling. The sight was so upsetting to the women that they bowed their faces to the ground.

Who were these two angels, and did they fit the symbolism of the others? In the Holy of Holies of Solomon's Temple were two statues of cherubim.

> In the inner sanctuary he made two cherubim 15 feet high out of olive wood. One wing of the [first] cherub was seven and a half feet long, and the other wing was seven and a half feet long. The wingspan was 15 feet from tip to tip. The second cherub also was 15 feet; both cherubim had the same size and shape. The first cherub's height was

> 15 feet and so was the second cherub's. Then he put the cherubim inside the inner temple. Since their wings were spread out, the first one's wing touched [one] wall while the second cherub's wing touched the other wall, and in the middle of the temple their wings were touching wing to wing. He also overlaid the cherubim with gold. (1 Kings 6:23–28)

These two beings represented the other angels in the Holy of Holies, the fifteen-foot-tall statues whose wings overshadowed the ark of the covenant with its two cherubim. Their dazzling clothing, their stunning appearance mirror the reflective quality of the gold that covered the olive wood statues.

One more angel was present that morning, and his appearance was the most dramatic of all. "After the Sabbath, as the first day of the week was dawning, Mary Magdalene and the other Mary went to view the tomb. Suddenly there was a violent earthquake, because an angel of the Lord descended from heaven and approached [the tomb]. He rolled back the stone and was sitting on it. His appearance was like lightning, and his robe was as white as snow" (Matt. 28:1–3).

There is no confusion in this passage. Matthew told us straight out "an angel of the Lord descended." His appearance was breathtaking and like some of the other angels in the tomb, he was seen sitting but outside the tomb and on the stone that sealed Jesus in.

Who was this angel, or whom did he represent? We are not told, but Matthew recorded some details that can't be overlooked. A list of those details looks like this:

1. Sudden and violent earthquake
2. Earthquake attributed to the arrival of the angel
3. The angel "descended" from heaven.
4. The angel described as approaching the tomb.
5. The angel rolled back the stone and sat on it.
6. His appearance was "like lightning."
7. His garment was "white as snow."

The earthquake mentioned was the second in three days. Matthew stated, "The earth quaked and the rocks were split" as Christ hung dying on the cross (27:51b). Now, another quake rumbled through the area, and Matthew tied it to the descent of the angel of the Lord, a quake he described as violent (literally, "great" from *megas*).

In Scripture, earthquakes are often associated with the judgment or the presence of God.[3] When God descended on Mount Sinai (note the descending aspect), "the whole mountain shook violently" (Exod. 19:18). At the punishment of Korah and his people, the ground not only shook but opened beneath the feet of the rebels who challenged God and his chosen leader. After the prophet Elijah fled from the evil Jezebel, he hid on a mountain and God "appeared" as wind, fire, earthquake, and then as a small voice.

The angel's appearance was unique. Matthew used a term for appearance that appears only here in the New Testament (*eidea*). It refers to the form, the physical aspect of the person. This angel had the external form of lightning. If this seems familiar, it should. Light and lightning are often associated with God. Lightning is often associated with the appearance of God.

As we saw with earthquakes, lightning accompanied the descent of the Lord on Mount Sinai. "On the third day, when morning came, there was thunder and lightning, a thick cloud on the mountain, and a loud trumpet sound, so that all the people in the camp shuddered" (Exod. 19:16). Interesting that this happened on the third day.

Ezekiel had several amazing and frightening visions of God. In one he saw lightning coming from the throne of the Almighty. And he saw creatures "darting back and forth like flashes of lightning" (Ezek. 1:14).

The apostle John described flashes of lightning coming from the throne of God (Rev. 4:5a). He also wrote: "God's sanctuary in heaven was opened, and the ark of His covenant appeared in His sanctuary. There were lightnings, rumblings, thunders, an earthquake, and severe hail" (Rev. 11:19).

Matthew described the angel's clothing as being whiter than snow. Each of the angels, regardless of what term the Gospel writer used to describe them, wore clothing that ranged from white to "dazzling." This angel was no different.

White is associated with the presence of God. Moses' face glowed white after being on the mountain with God. On the Mount of Transfiguration, Jesus was changed physically and his clothing became a brilliant white. The three Gospels that record the event use different terms to say the same thing. Matthew: "Even His clothes became as white as the light" (17:2b). Mark: "And His clothes became dazzling [from the same root word used for lightning]—extremely white as no launderer on earth could whiten them" (9:3). And Luke: "His clothes became dazzling white" (9:29b).

Who then was this angel? We can't say for certain, but considering at the very least the description and careful use of terms as well as what the other angels represented, we can conclude that he represented God's presence and may even have been what theologians call a theophany—God, who is spirit, appearing to someone in physical form.

Charting the details found in the Gospels, we see an interesting pattern:

Gospel	Term	Number	Location	Position	Seen by
Matthew 28:1-7	An angel (angelos x 2)	One	Outside	Seated on stone	Women
Mark 16:1-7	Young man (neaniskos)	One	Inside	Seated "on right"	Women
Luke 24:1-8	Men (aner)	Two	Inside	Standing (suddenly)	Women
John 20:1-18	Angels (angelos)	Two	Seen inside	Seated at head and foot of bier	Mary Magdalene

Putting It All Together

Taking the Gospel accounts together provides an interesting and stunning picture. The tomb was more than an empty vessel that held the body of Jesus for a short time. It became something symbolic and taught a lesson more powerful than words can ever hope to do.

A short distance from the tomb, beyond the walls that surrounded Jerusalem, in the heart of the city stood the magnificent structure called the temple. It was the second temple and third variation of the original built by Solomon. Herod—the same king who had the babies in Bethlehem put to death in an effort to kill the infant Christ—had enlarged the grounds and made the structure as grand as any ever built.

Inside that temple priests had made, and would again make, blood sacrifices for the sins of the people. That would end in AD 70 when the Romans would tear it to the ground, leaving only one retaining wall in place—the present-day Wailing Wall.

Although the sacrificial practices would continue for several more decades, their usefulness died when Jesus did, and his resurrection put to rest the need for any more sacrifice. The author of Hebrews put it this way: "He [Jesus] entered the holy of holies once for all, not by the blood of goats and calves, but by His own blood, having obtained eternal redemption" (9:12).

When did Jesus enter the Holy of Holies? The people who knew him understood him to be a rabbi but not a priest, let alone the high priest who once a year entered the most holy place. Is this verse hyperbole, speech exaggerated for effect, or is it much more? Was the author of Hebrews referring to something else—to the borrowed tomb of Christ?

When Jesus died on the cross, the nine-inch-thick curtain that sealed off the Holy of Holies was torn from top to bottom (Matt. 27:51), throwing open the previously secret room. The imagery is that the temple's holiest room was no longer needed. Why? Because the final sacrifice for humankind took place on the cross and his body was laid in a different Holy of Holies.

The angels in and around the tomb were a living portrait of a timeless truth. Christ became our sacrifice, entered the Holy of Holies that we call his tomb, and rose from the dead as final but now a living sacrifice for humankind.

John 20:11–12. "But Mary stood outside facing the tomb, crying. As she was crying, she stooped to look into the tomb. She saw two angels in white sitting there, one at the head and one at the feet, where Jesus' body had been lying."

Luke 24:4. "While they were perplexed about this, suddenly two men stood by them in dazzling clothes."

Mark 16:5. "When they entered the tomb, they saw a young man dressed in a long white robe sitting on the right side; they were amazed and alarmed."

Matthew 28:2. "Suddenly there was a violent earthquake, because an angel of the Lord descended from heaven and approached [the tomb]. He rolled back the stone and was sitting on it."

Part 2

From the Tomb to the World

*"Listen! We are going up to Jerusalem.
The Son of Man will be handed over to the chief priests and scribes, and they will condemn Him to death. Then they will hand Him over to the Gentiles to be mocked, flogged, and crucified, and He will be resurrected on the third day."*

—MATTHEW 20:18–19

Christ himself deliberately staked his whole claim to the credit of men upon his resurrection. When asked for a sign he pointed to this sign as his single and sufficient credential.

—B. B. WARFIELD

Chapter 6

Encounter with Mary

As the sun crawled beyond the horizon, as a spring dawn breeze blew through the garden, as the dark of night melted away, came one of the most unique women in history. Her steps were rushed, her gait uneven, and her heart a shambles.

The image is as poignant as any ever witnessed. Though others would join her, she stood alone in her emotions. Mary Magdalene was about to become the most unique person ever to live. To her had been given an honor not offered to Peter or John who had been at the same spot not long before.

Mary of Magdala would be the first human to see the resurrected Jesus.

> But Mary stood outside facing the tomb, crying. As she was crying, she stooped to look into the tomb. She saw two angels in white sitting there, one at the head and one at the feet, where

Jesus' body had been lying. They said to her, "Woman, why are you crying?"

"Because they've taken away my Lord," she told them, "and I don't know where they've put Him." Having said this, she turned around and saw Jesus standing there, though she did not know it was Jesus.

"Woman," Jesus said to her, "why are you crying? Who is it you are looking for?"

Supposing He was the gardener, she replied, "Sir, if you've removed Him, tell me where you've put Him, and I will take Him away."

Jesus said, "Mary."

Turning around, she said to Him in Hebrew, "Rabbouni!"—which means "Teacher."

"Don't cling to Me," Jesus told her, "for I have not yet ascended to the Father. But go to My brothers and tell them that I am ascending to My Father and your Father—to My God and your God."

Mary Magdalene went and announced to the disciples, "I have seen the Lord!" And she told them what He had said to her. (John 20:11–18)

The Actors

The Mysterious and Misunderstood Mary of Magdala

The garden in which the borrowed tomb of Christ was located served as a dynamic venue for the events that played there. Like a fine theatrical play, the stage had been set. A tomb that should have held the mortal remains of the rabbi from Galilee stood open, the large stone door rolled to the side. The grass and soil were still damp from the night's condensation. The perfume of flowers and trees hung in the air.

The first actor in this real drama moved to the open maw of the sepulcher. Her heart was mutilated by the events of days before when the One she admired, respected, followed, and loved hung battered on the cross and died.

Tears stained her face, her body was weighed down with grief and now, at seeing the empty tomb, with mind-numbing shock and disbelief.

Who was this woman who came to shed her grief and found more grief instead? Her name is Mary, Miriam in Hebrew, a woman of means from the Galilean town of Magdala (also known as Magadan), on the western shore of the Sea of Galilee. We have very few facts about her, but ironically, we have many myths.

Mary was one of six[1] people by that name in the New Testament. Her role was pivotal but often underrated. She was one of the least understood and most misrepresented people of the Bible.

Luke gave us the greatest insight: "Soon afterwards He was traveling from one town and village to another, preaching and telling the good news of the kingdom of God. The Twelve were with Him, and also some women who had been healed of evil spirits and sicknesses: Mary, called Magdalene (seven demons had come out of her); Joanna the wife of Chuza, Herod's steward; Susanna; and many others who were supporting them from their possessions" (8:1–3).

For a time in her life, Mary was possessed by seven demons. Not one but seven. This fact conjures up the image of the man possessed by numerous demons who identified themselves as Legion because they were so many (Mark 5:9b).

Exorcism was part of Jesus' ministry. "So He went into all of Galilee, preaching in their synagogues and driving out demons" (Mark 1:39). Apparently, Jesus did so many of these that we have only a representative sample of the events. How and when Jesus cast the demons out of Mary Magdalene is unknown, only that he did it. But unlike many who were healed and returned to their daily lives, Mary Magdalene and some other women became sponsors of Jesus' ministry, supporting him and his disciples from their private possessions. In some ways, these women were the female versions of the disciples. It seems that Mary Magdalene was the leader of the band of women.

Mary was a woman of great courage. She followed Jesus in his ministry all the way to the cross and to the tomb. It was a long journey. As a demon-possessed person, she must have been a desperate woman, and on her release she threw her heart into the support of Jesus' ministry.

One of the myths surrounding Mary Magdalene is that she was a prostitute. Nothing in Scripture indicates this. Some think she should be identified with the woman in Luke 7:36–50. Perhaps this is because those verses immediately precede those about Mary, beginning in Luke 8. This myth is so persistent that it led to the coining of the term "a magdalene"—a former or repentant prostitute.

Others have suggested she was Jesus' consort, lover, and even his wife who bore his children. There is no evidence for such nonsense. Some have called on ancient books that supposedly were written by the apostles. The Gospel of

Philip states Mary was Christ's consort and that he kissed her frequently. So great was his ardor that others around them became jealous.[2] The Gospel of Thomas has Peter requesting that Mary be sent away because women are not worthy of life, so Jesus promised to make her male.[3] Neither of these books are considered by scholars to be inspired and were not included in the canon of Scripture. Even a casual reading by someone familiar with the Bible shows the lack of spiritual weight to them.

Mary was a woman of means healed by Jesus, a woman who found truth in him. She was a faithful supporter who stood in the garish shadow of the cross and deserves better attention than she gets. While myth and speculation abound, the New Testament reveals her to be a heroine of the faith. She worked no miracles, wrote no books, preached no messages, but her life and steel-like courage are an inspiration.

She had the courage to invest her life and resources in Jesus and to stand at the foot of the cross when his other followers had scattered. She watched the sword pierce her Savior's side.

When Jesus died, her world died with him.

Heartbroken, she headed to the tomb, only to face another indignity. To her mind, the grave had been defiled and the body of Christ stolen. It was no wonder she was in tears.

Listening to Angels

We have already seen the importance and symbolism of the two angels seated on the bier where Jesus' body had been laid to rest, but they did more than serve as an object lesson for Mary. They were actors on the same stage.

Angels were frequently associated with key events in Christ's life. Angels announced his birth to shepherds and ministered to him at the end of his temptations in the wilderness; an angel was in the Garden of Gethsemane, and angels were present at the Resurrection.

These angels were the first messengers of the Resurrection.

The Star of the Show

One other actor was on the stage, the One everyone came to see. Jesus appeared, seemingly out of nowhere, and we get our first glimpse at the resurrected Savior.

The Drama

Years ago, I was asked to direct a community stage play. It was something I had wanted to do, so I leaped at the chance. As I studied the script, I had to analyze dialogue, plot the movement of actors, consider backdrops and stage props, and fill the cast. It was a fascinating process but filled with more detail than I imagined. I soon realized I had to reduce the story to its basic elements. As a writer, it was easy for me to do. All story is about conflict and resolution. The conflict can be subtle or overpowering, but as every storyteller knows, if there is no conflict, internal or otherwise, there is no story and resolution is meaningless.

Although the sun was rising, Mary was living in darkness. Jesus had been killed in the most horrible fashion, hastily buried, and was now missing from his borrowed tomb. What was Mary to think? What was she to do?

She did the expected. She wept. This passage contains

the word *crying* four times. Other translations use the stronger term *weeping.* The original word (*klaio*) means to weep aloud, to wail, to cry out. Mary wasn't merely shedding a few tears, she was crying audibly. Think of the Middle Eastern culture in which wailing is encouraged at funerals. In Jesus' day professional mourners could be hired to weep publicly for the departed. If we stood by her side, we would have heard the deep sobs erupting from a shattered heart. She had been deprived of the simple dignity of proper grief and was left with nothing but an open tomb.

Her confusion must have been profound. First, she saw confusing things: open tomb, angels, the empty wrappings of Jesus, and the missing guards.

She thought confusing things: *Someone stole the body. Who are these men in the tomb? What should I do now?*

Then she heard confusing things: a question asked twice. "Woman, why are you crying?" the angels asked. Then moments later, Jesus asked the same thing.

Here the drama made an unexpected turn. At some point and in some fashion we're not told, Jesus appeared. "Having said this," the text says, "she turned around and saw Jesus standing there." What caused her to turn? How long had he been behind her?

Whatever the answer, the next revelation causes the mind to seize. She doesn't recognize him. Mary, who traveled with Jesus, supported him financially, watched him die, did not recognize him. She first concluded that Jesus was the gardener, the one responsible for the enclosed area.

Many reasons have been suggested for why Mary could not recognize Jesus. Some have suggested her vision was limited because of her tears, but she seemed to have no problem seeing the angels inside the dark tomb. Did the change from the dim light of the tomb to the bright light of morning prevent her from seeing clearly? Perhaps, but such suggestions don't satisfy the text. There was something different about Jesus.

Not only did she not recognize his appearance, but she didn't identify his voice, a voice she must have heard countless times.

Jesus asked two puzzling questions. First, "Woman, why are you crying?" With an open tomb nearby, the answer seems obvious. This was less a question than a statement. Mary's tears revealed her understanding, or lack of understanding, about Jesus' teaching of his resurrection. Standing as we do two thousand years removed from the moment, we might be tempted to be critical of Mary for not believing what Jesus had taught about his death and resurrection, but her crime was the same as that committed by the disciples. If we were living then, we, too, would have found it hard to believe. Jesus, through this question, was reminding her that this was no normal situation. There was no reason to weep.

His second question also seems unnecessary: "Who is it you are looking for?" Jesus knew whom she was searching for, but she longed for what didn't exist. Mary wanted to know where the dead body of Jesus had been taken, but there was no body to be found. That is the point of the Resurrection. The "who" of the question stood before her.

Still, Mary didn't make the connection. Lost in grief, she wasn't able to look beyond the moment. Then Jesus uttered one word—her name.

Maybe it was the way he said it. Perhaps it was something in the intonation or spoken in a way that only she would recognize. In whatever manner he said it, it did the trick.

"Rabbouni!" exploded from her lips, and she seized his feet in joy. *Rabbi* means teacher. He called her by her given name, and she called him by his work. Her teacher stood alive and well. At that point nothing else mattered. She had eyes only for Jesus. Forgotten were the angels, the tomb, the guards, and the sorrow.

Mary turned from facing the tomb of a dead man to seeing a very living Jesus. She had come to mourn her teacher and found a Savior instead.

There is something special about this revelation. No king, no leader, no person of great prominence would announce something so important to a woman first. Not in the culture of that day. No Jewish author fabricating a tale would conceive of a woman being the first to witness the world's most surprising event. Yet, that is exactly what happened here. Mary came looking for Jesus, and he found her.

The Outcome

Joy replaced Mary's weeping. Out of the worst came the very best. That overpowering release of pain and the inrush of relief compelled Mary to take hold of Jesus as if never to let him go again. No doubt she would have been content to spend the rest of her days holding the feet of the One she had shed so many tears over, but Jesus was going to leave again.

"Don't cling to me," Jesus told her, "for I have not yet ascended to the Father."

There was more to be done. Jesus would appear several more times over the next forty days and then ascend to heaven. Mary also had a job to do: "But go to My brothers and tell them that I am ascending to My Father and your Father—to My God and your God."

What personal statements. First, Jesus sent this woman to preach the first ever Easter message, and she was to preach it to the disciples, the men Jesus graciously called "My brothers." Then he paired his Father with hers (and all believers'): "My Father and your Father—to My God and your God."

It may have been the shortest sermon ever preached. The Resurrection means the blockade of sin that kept us from fellowship with our Creator, our Father, our God, has been moved away just as the stone door was pushed to the side.

Joseph of Arimathea and Nicodemus left a corpse in a tomb; Mary was holding the ankles of a very living Savior. In those moments, knowledge replaced ignorance. Now it all made sense. Everything Jesus taught about the events of the past few days came into sharp focus. Like cockroaches, doubts flee in the presence of light. The tearful, crushed Mary now understood.

The Mary Lesson

At the epicenter of history stood a woman who had suffered at the hands of evil itself, her body a vessel for demons—a woman, although well-to-do, who because of her gender could only stand in the penumbra of social influence; a woman with a mind branded by the heart-shredding image of the battered Christ on the cross; a woman reduced to a wailing, empty shell, became the one chosen to first deliver a message previously only given by angels.

Mary Magdalene, misunderstood by history, tainted by myth and bad scholarship, remained the choice of God to be the first to touch the body of the risen Christ, to hear his voice and to stare into his eyes.

It was in the early 1920s when Nikolay Ivanovich Bukharin traveled from Moscow to Kiev to deliver a speech at an anti-God rally. For over an hour, he railed against Christianity, ridiculing faith and belief. At the end he asked if there were questions. A Russian Orthodox priest stepped forward, faced the large crowd, and gave the Easter greeting common in Orthodox churches, "He is risen!" Immediately the people rose to their feet and shouted back, "He is risen, indeed." The point was made with a simple statement.

There have been those who cast doubt on the physical resurrection of Jesus, dismissing it as myth or superstition. For Mary, it was a tangible fact, and it has remained so for every believer since.

Theologian Herschel Hobbs noted that after the Resurrection, no enemy ever visited the tomb. Why? Fear. After Mary, there was no recorded visit to the tomb by any friend of Jesus. Why? Knowledge. He was not there.

Chapter 7

The Women Came First

Some of the greatest things to happen to us come by way of surprise. When I went to college, I went looking for a degree, not a wife. I got the wife before I got the degree.

A wonderful surprise.

When I was a young husband, I learned I was to be a young father. Somewhat surprising, but not nearly so much as when Becky returned home from a doctor's visit and said, "The doctor thinks we might be having twins."

A wonderful surprise!

Mary Magdalene was the first to see the resurrected Christ, and no more wonderful a surprise can be found. But it appears she wasn't alone. While John emphasized Mary, Matthew, Mark, and Luke mention other women there with Mary or arriving soon after she returned to the tomb.

Taking the names mentioned in the four Gospels, we get a partial list of those who gathered at the tomb.

We met Mary Magdalene in the last chapter and learned of her past and her strength and dismissed the groundless myths that surround her. Her presence at the tomb is recorded in all four Gospels, something unique to her.

Another Mary was present. Matthew called her "the other Mary" (28:1). Mark and Luke referred to her as "Mary the mother of James" (Mark 16:1; Luke 24:10). Earlier in his book, Mark described her as "Mary the mother of James the younger and of Joses" (Mark 15:40). She was present at the Crucifixion (Matt. 27:55–56) and sat with Mary Magdalene at the tomb (Matt. 27:61). John described her first as sister to Mary the mother of Jesus and then as "wife of Clopas" (John 19:25). The word "wife" is not in the original language but is assumed from the grammar. Her description as the sister of Jesus' mother gets a little confusing. It means Mary had a sister named Mary. Not impossible but unlikely. Perhaps Mary the wife of Clopas was a sister-in-law. Whatever the family relationship, she was a follower of Christ through the bitter end. (It is an interesting irony that there were three individuals named Mary at the cross.)

Also arriving at the tomb was Salome (Mark 16:1). Her name is the feminine version of Solomon. She was also among the brave band of women at the cross (Mark 15:40).

The fourth woman named was Joanna (Luke 24:10), "the wife of Chuza, Herod's steward" (Luke 8:3). Interesting that the wife of one of Herod Antipas's house stewards would be a disciple of Christ and a financial contributor. Before his crucifixion, Jesus stood before Herod and was treated with contempt. One wonders whether Chuza watched the kangaroo court and told his wife of the events.

Luke mentioned "the other women with them" (Luke 24:10). How many women this phrase refers to is unknown. We do know that four women are mentioned by name and that several more came to the tomb that Sunday morning.

Their Objective

I admire their courage. We have to remember Jesus was taken by force and that he had many enemies. The danger to his followers was so real that many of them went into hiding. When Joseph of Arimathea went to Pilate to request the right to take Jesus' body, he did so "but secretly because of his fear of the Jews" (John 19:38). His fear was universal among disciples. John, who was there, recorded, "In the evening of that first day of the week, the disciples were gathered together with the doors locked because of their fear of the Jews" (20:19).

It was an easy exercise of logic to realize that now that Jesus was dead, his disciples would be next. Nonetheless, despite sadness in their hearts and fear in their minds, a handful of women went to the burial place of Christ.

Why run the risk? It was customary to visit the grave of a loved one for thirty days, but they had more on their minds. The burial of Christ had been rushed. In their minds, proper burial activities might have been overlooked. So they "bought spices, so they could go and anoint Him" (Mark 16:1).

They could not save his life, but they could treat him well in death. As we have seen, Nicodemus took and, with the help of Joseph of Arimathea, used seventy-five pounds of burial spices. Perhaps the women brought other types of spices to add to the work already done.

Not knowing what the guards would do, uncertain how to move the large stone, they went anyway. Love compelled them to face whatever came.

Women on a Mission

Death was a frequent visitor to first-century people. The median age of death was substantially lower than in our Western world. These women knew what to expect. They anticipated a three-day-old corpse, funeral wrappings, and a dark tomb.

What they got was a surprise:

> On the first day of the week, very early in the morning, they came to the tomb, bringing the spices they had prepared. They found the stone rolled away from the tomb. They went in but did not find the body of the Lord Jesus. While they were perplexed about this, suddenly two men stood by them in dazzling clothes. So the women were terrified and bowed down to the ground.
>
> "Why are you looking for the living among the dead?" asked the men. "He is not here, but He has been resurrected! Remember how He spoke to you when He was still in Galilee, saying, 'The Son of Man must be betrayed into the hands of sinful men, be crucified, and rise on the third day'?" And they remembered His words.

> Returning from the tomb, they reported all these things to the Eleven and to all the rest. Mary Magdalene, Joanna, Mary the mother of James, and the other women with them were telling the apostles these things. (Luke 24:1–10)

Approaching the empty tomb, the women entered and were stunned to discover the body of Jesus was missing. Before they had time to react, a pair of men in dazzling clothes appeared with a question: "Why are you looking for the living among the dead?" The question was as dazzling as the men's apparel. It was more a statement than question. As if anticipating the women's questions, they told the women Jesus was not in the grave. The messengers then jogged the women's memory: "Remember how He spoke to you when He was still in Galilee, saying, 'The Son of Man must be betrayed into the hands of sinful men, be crucified, and rise on the third day'?"

The reminder explained it all. Jesus promised to rise from the dead.

Matthew included additional details. "So, departing quickly from the tomb with fear and great joy, they ran to tell His disciples the news. Just then Jesus met them and said, 'Good morning!' They came up, took hold of His feet, and worshiped Him. Then Jesus told them, 'Do not be afraid. Go and tell My brothers to leave for Galilee, and they will see Me there'" (28:8–10).

Perhaps only those who have experienced deep loss can imagine what it must have been like for these women to see not a corpse but a living Savior. This time there seemed to be no confusion about his identity.

The way Jesus behaved is important. He greeted them with the typical greeting of the day, "Good morning!" He walked, talked, gave instruction, and allowed himself to be touched.

And touch was what the women did. They bowed, took hold of Jesus' feet, and worshiped. This last act was important. An onlooker not familiar with what had occurred would consider the sight blasphemous, worthy of death, but the women worshiped Jesus as God without hesitation—and Jesus allowed it.

Then Jesus turned the stunned women into messengers. He gave them the privilege of taking word of his resurrection to those who knew him best. The response the women received was disappointing: "But these words seemed like nonsense to them [the apostles], and they did not believe the women" (Luke 24:11).

A Storm of Emotions

Today the Resurrection event is celebrated on Easter, a day named after the ancient Anglo-Saxon goddess of spring and fertility, Eastre. The day is associated with colored eggs, bunnies, Easter dresses, and bonnets. Churches hold sunrise services and call their worship services "celebrations" and rightly so. The Resurrection should be celebrated. There is no more important day, but the first experience with Christ's resurrection was far more emotional than most realize. So complex was the emotional stew the women felt that each Gospel writer used a different set of terms to describe the experience.

Matthew said they felt fear. He used the word *phobos,* from which we get our term *phobia.* It is a stark, often sudden, fear like what someone with a fear of spiders feels when one of the eight-legged creatures crawls over his hand. These women did not just feel fear, they were impacted by it.

But then Matthew added another feeling: "great joy." The word he used (*chara*) means cheer and delight. These are oil and water emotions. In the same moment they felt spine-tingling fear and heart-racing joy. They had one foot in boiling water and the other in ice water; the sight of Jesus was that astounding.

Mark said they were "amazed and alarmed." Several translations use two words here, but there is only one in the original. It's a difficult word to match to a single English term. They were completely astonished and fully amazed. He then described them as trembling (*thromos*). This is a physical response. The shock was so intense they quaked in their sandals.

Mark wasn't done. He further described the women as overwhelmed with astonishment. The term he used is *exstasis,* which means to be moved out of place. News and sights of the Resurrection displaced their thoughts and emotions, which explains the last term Mark used: afraid (from *ephobounto*). And it was a fear that stayed with them for some time.

Dr. Luke fleshed out the emotional quagmire even more, adding that the ladies were "perplexed" and "terrified." The word translated "perplexed" (*aporeo*) paints the picture of someone at a loss and without the resources to deal with what has just been seen and heard.

As we saw in the chapter on Mary Magdalene, she was weeping (*klaio*) and wailing.

All those emotions came on the women in a single wave. No wonder they were staggered, knocked back on their heels. Time has dimmed the emotions we feel when we celebrate the Resurrection. Secular contrivances and conveniences have removed the stunning shock of what happened so long ago. To be fair, it is impossible for us who dwell in the twenty-first century to experience what those special women did on that first Resurrection Sunday; but it does remind us that the Resurrection shook the world, by shaking one person at a time.

The Resurrection is emotional stuff. It started that way, and it remains so. History turned on the event; eternity is built on the foundation of what happened that day.

When we gaze back through the centuries, we face the same impossible truth the brave women saw; it is no less moving today. It was not an isolated historical event but the most important fact in every believer's life, transcending place and time.

The stone rolled away from the tomb, and the gate to eternity opened. Every time we look back to the event, a two-thousand-year-old bolt of lightning strikes the heart, soul, and mind. There is no wonder these women experienced such a wide range of emotions, from the highest joy to crippling fear.

Unexpected Encounter

"Just then Jesus met them and said, 'Good morning!' They came up, took hold of His feet, and worshiped Him.

Then Jesus told them, 'Do not be afraid. Go and tell My brothers to leave for Galilee, and they will see Me there'" (Matt. 28:9–10).

These women had come to the tomb on a mission: to anoint the dead. Instead, they encountered the living. It is significant that Jesus met them and not the other way around. In the midst of the emotional storm brought on by the empty tomb and the sudden appearances of otherworldly beings, Jesus sought them out.

No one knows exactly where this meeting took place. The text tells us the women "ran" (Matt. 28:8) to deliver word to the disciples. Somewhere along the path, Jesus appeared.

Why? Weren't they on their way to spread the news of what they had seen and heard? It seems the women were already convinced. Yet Jesus took the time to appear. Did they need more convincing? Doubtful. Seeing and talking to angels were convincing enough.

The answer is revealed in Jesus' comments. First, he greeted them: "Good morning!" but Jesus said more than that. The term he used (*charete*) is a command to rejoice. In this context it takes on a special meaning, because Jesus' next command was for them to cease their fear.

Fear is a crippling emotion that fogs the mind and hinders faith. Jesus wanted them to know there was nothing to fear. What they saw was real, not imagined; what they heard was true and not a lie. The command not to fear was first uttered by the angels, but hearing it from Jesus raised the command to new heights.

Christ's sudden appearance achieved something else: it lent credibility to the message the women were to deliver. While the description of the empty tomb and the appearance of angels were as dramatic as anything the world has seen, being able to say, "I saw Jesus!" was far more powerful.

Spreading the Word

In the midst of a storm of fear and confusion, Jesus chose to reveal himself. The women did what any believer would do when standing toe to toe with Jesus—they fell to the ground and worshiped.

Jesus then gave them orders that seem to be identical with those issued by the angels: "Go and tell My brothers to leave for Galilee, and they will see Me there." But is it identical? Most assume that Jesus' reference to "My brothers" is a euphemism for the disciples. That may be the case, but there was more to the statement.

If the women went to the disciples as instructed by the angel (Matt. 28:7) and the disciples immediately left for Galilee, then their first encounter with the risen Christ would have been in that northern region, but it wasn't. As we will see, Jesus appeared to them in Jerusalem before he appeared to them in Galilee.

There are two additional possibilities here. First, Jesus was speaking of his literal brothers. The Bible lists four people as the brothers of Jesus: James, Joseph, Simon, and Judas—not to be confused with the disciples with the same names (Matt. 13:55). They also appear in John 7:1–8. During his ministry, Jesus' brothers remained unbelievers (John 7:5). However, they would come around after the Resurrection. "All these were continually united in prayer, along with the women, including Mary the mother of Jesus, and his brothers" (Acts 1:14). Whether these brothers were the offspring of Mary after Jesus' birth or part of Joseph's family from a previous marriage (some believe Joseph was a widower) is immaterial. There is no biblical reason to think Mary didn't have other children. The perpetual virginity of Mary is not a biblical doctrine.

It appears that Jesus was broadening the angel's command to include not only the disciples but also Jesus' half brothers. At least two of the brothers become pillars in the church. James would succeed Peter as head of the church and later die a martyr's death. He was the author of the New Testament book James.

Judas (also known as Jude) would pen the little but powerful book of Jude, which challenges Gnosticism and false teaching.

Jesus was making certain his unbelieving brothers had opportunity to see him. It was an event that forever changed their lives and ours. The Resurrection turned them from unbelievers into church leaders.

There may have been even a wider group in Jesus' mind—the five hundred. Paul wrote to the church at Corinth about the importance of the Resurrection. In his defense of the historical event, he checked off a list of those who witnessed the risen Savior, which includes this line: "Then He appeared to over 500 brothers at one time, most of whom remain to the present, but some have fallen asleep" (1 Cor. 15:6). Interesting that Paul would call them "brothers." It's also fair to wonder how these five hundred heard of the monumental event or how they knew where to meet and when. Certainly news would have spread among the followers by word of mouth, but it may have been Mary Magdalene, Mary the mother of James, Salome, Joanna, and the select other women who became town criers.

Of course, all three scenarios could be true. The women not only told the disciples but made certain that Jesus' brothers and the whole Christian community knew of the Resurrection.

There is a comforting joy in seeing Jesus honor the faithful women by making them the first to see him resurrected, then sending them on a mission to tell his brothers that death could not hold him.

Why Women?

In human history, the two greatest events are Creation and the death/resurrection of Jesus. All of Christianity hinges on the latter. If there is no Resurrection, Christianity is a hollow shell of belief and Jesus is just another prophet. That leads to a nagging question: Why women?

Why appear to the women first? It was Peter who led the early church. The other disciples started an evangelistic explosion never matched in history. All but one of the original disciples died martyrs' deaths; and John, the only to not die of persecution, would suffer immeasurably and endure exile. Shouldn't such dedication be rewarded by being the first to see Jesus? Peter and John were at the tomb, indeed, entered the tomb, but Jesus did not appear to them as he did to Mary and the other women. Why?

Specific answers aren't given, but there are several possibilities. First, they were there. It appears that Peter and John stayed only long enough to enter the empty tomb and observe the strange state of the wrappings and then left, believing but confused. It seems the women stayed longer. Still, while that may be a factor, it doesn't seem a solid enough reason.

One reason that they may have been the first to see the risen Jesus was the kind of testimony they could give. If Peter and some of the other men claimed to have seen Jesus first, the enemies of the faith might have accused them of perpetrating a plot. Steal the body, dispose of it, and then claim a resurrection.

These women could not be accused of having such an agenda. In the first century, women could do many things but were still very limited by today's standards. Jewish society was far more limiting to women than Roman, yet they still played an important role in society. By New Testament times, women could divorce their husbands (Mark 10:12), hold prominence in the early church (Prisca, Rom. 16:3), be a servant/deacon as in the case of Phoebe (Rom. 16:1), own and operate a business as Lydia did in Thyatira (Acts 16:14, 40), and possess wealth as these women did, wealth they used to support the ministry of Jesus.

Christianity was the first great gender equalizer. Paul wrote, "There is no Jew or Greek, slave or free, male or female; for you are all one in Christ Jesus" (Gal. 3:28). Women suffered persecution for their faith. Pliny the Younger wrote to the Emperor Trajan, "Accordingly, I judged it all the more necessary to find out what the truth was by torturing two female slaves who were called deaconesses. But I discovered nothing else but depraved, excessive superstition."[1]

While there had been some change in the status of women by New Testament times, Jewish women still lived in the shadow of men. Ironically, this limited status may have made Mary and the other women better witnesses. To outsiders, these women had nothing to gain in speaking of the Resurrection.

Also, those who had witnessed the Crucifixion—and since crucifixion was a public affair, a great many did—would know that these woman had been at the foot of the cross. Only one male of note, John, was there. The testimony of these women could be, "I was close enough to touch him when he died. I know he was dead. Now I know he is alive again."

These women had traveled in the shadows of Jesus' ministry, doing what they could and providing financial support. Now they were thrust into the limelight among the other believers as having been chosen to receive the honor of hearing the angelic announcement, then seeing and touching the resurrected Savior.

Jesus rewarded their faithfulness, and now they stand unique in the pages of history.

Chapter 8

Peter's Secret Meeting

In the world of politics and business, secret meetings are the norm. Some things are not meant for the eyes and ears of others, so executives meet behind closed doors and world leaders exchange cryptic communiqués. Most of the recorded appearances of Christ come packed with details. When we read them, we get a sense of place and action. With Mary Magdalene in the garden, we see her weeping before the open and empty tomb. But two of the appearances shatter that pattern. Christ's appearance to Peter is one of those cases.

So thin are the details of this event it is easy to overlook that it even happened. There are no details. We don't know the place. We have no idea of the time (although it appears to have occurred after Jesus' appearance to the women and before his appearance to the two men on the road to Emmaus). No dialogue was recorded; and there were, to the best of our knowledge, no other witnesses to the event. Yet, this secret meeting is referred to twice in the pages of the New Testament.

The third appearance of Christ was to a special and a unique man. We know him best by the name Peter. What makes this appearance so interesting is not what has been revealed but what has been kept secret. Peter is the only one of the Eleven to receive a private audience with the King.

Why secret? Why no account of the close encounter?

Because it was personal.

Peter, of all the disciples, was the most vocal. He was the extrovert's extrovert. A man of passion and commitment, he loved Jesus deeply, but that passion and love crumbled like chalk.

I believe Jesus had a private meeting with Peter to set things right. This was no public penance. Reconciliation was private.

The Man with Many Names

The first time we read through the Gospels, we notice Peter was a man with more than one name. In a multi language society, this wasn't unusual. If we had lived during the first century, we would have heard Hebrew spoken in religious settings, Greek in business situations, Latin when dealing with the Romans, and Aramaic in everyday conversation. Peter's various names were tied to the languages of his day.

Simon comes from the Hebrew *Simeon* and means "God hears." On the other hand, *Cephas* is an Aramaic term from *Kephas* and means a "rock" or "stone." *Peter* is the Greek version of the Aramaic. It also means "rock."

In the Gospel of Matthew is a one-on-one exchange

between Peter and Jesus. Jesus has asked the disciples what the prevailing belief was about his identity. They gave him several, then Jesus made it personal asking who they, the disciples, believed him to be. Peter answered for the group when he said, "You are the Messiah, the Son of the living God!" (Matt. 16:16).

The answer thrilled Jesus. "And Jesus responded, 'Simon son of Jonah, you are blessed because flesh and blood did not reveal this to you, but My Father in heaven. And I also say to you that you are Peter, and on this rock I will build My church, and the forces of Hades will not overpower it. I will give you the keys of the kingdom of heaven, and whatever you bind on earth is already bound in heaven, and whatever you loose on earth is already loosed in heaven'" (Matt. 16:17–19).

Peter was a rock, but that sturdiness would soon crumble. Peter, who once claimed he would fight to the death for Jesus, would deny him in public.

Peter's Plummet

From that high moment when Jesus called Peter blessed came Peter's plummet to denial.

> While Peter was in the courtyard below, one of the high priest's servants came. When she saw Peter warming himself, she looked at him and said, "You also were with that Nazarene, Jesus."
>
> But he denied it: "I don't know or understand what you're talking about!" Then he went out to the entryway, and a rooster crowed.

> When the servant saw him again she began to tell those standing nearby, "This man is one of them!"
>
> But again he denied it. After a little while those standing there said to Peter again, "You certainly are one of them, since you're also a Galilean!"
>
> Then he started to curse and to swear with an oath, "I don't know this man you're talking about!"
>
> Immediately a rooster crowed a second time, and Peter remembered when Jesus had spoken the word to him, "Before the rooster crows twice, you will deny Me three times." When he thought about it, he began to weep. (Mark 14:66–72)

It was a short fall with a hard landing. Peter the bold and brash went down to denial and defeat, backed into a corner by a servant girl. His strength and leadership dissolved under the heat of questioning. To be sure, he was the only disciple who dared travel that close to Jesus after his arrest. Peter was in the courtyard of the high priest himself. He was alone and in the middle of enemy territory. That took courage.

"I will lay down my life for You!" Peter had boasted (John 13:37b); and at Jesus' arrest he did wade into the mob, cutting off a man's ear. Now, things had gone bad, and Peter could no longer muster the courage to publicly claim Christ. It would be wrong for us to cast blame on him. Who knows if we would have risked life and limb to travel as far as he did?

His denial included cursing, and he swore an oath. Cursing as it is used here was not the same as foul language. It was much more serious. What Peter did was place himself under a curse (*anathematizō*) that if he was lying about not knowing Jesus, God should strike him. A similar curse is found among a group of Jews who were out to kill the apostle Paul. "When it was day, the Jews formed a conspiracy and bound themselves under a curse: neither to eat nor to drink until they had killed Paul" (Acts 23:12).

Swearing in this passage means to take an oath before God that the lie was the truth. Although we don't have the actual words, Peter may have said something like, "I tell you before God that I do not know this Jesus, and may God punish me if I'm lying."

It was a good thing for Peter that God is patient.

We may withhold our criticism of Peter's denial, but Peter never withheld his own self-loathing. I doubt Peter ever recovered from what he did and said. Tradition states that Peter was crucified in Rome, but not feeling he deserved to die the same way as his Master, asked to be crucified upside down. If this is true, it must have been one of the oddest and extreme requests ever made. What could prompt a man to ask such a thing?

Guilt.

The hottest hate came from Peter himself. How do you face your friends, your family, yourself? How do you unwind the past? How do you draw back the words once they've been let loose?

None of us can say we would have done better. We weren't there. The pressure was enormous, the danger palpable, the sorrow overpowering.

When Judas betrayed Jesus and took money for the deed, he was surprised at the events that followed. He attempted to return the money, but when his religious conspirators refused to take it, he threw the thirty pieces of silver into the sanctuary, as if returning the money could ease his remorse (Matt. 27:3–10). It couldn't. Judas killed himself.

Peter never betrayed Jesus, but he did deny him—something that would haunt him all his days. Instead of killing himself, he returned to the other disciples and waited for events to unfold.

It was this emotionally mangled Peter that Jesus met in private.

Two Accounts with No Information

Guilt is an unbearable weight that grows heavier with time. What percolated in the damaged soul of Peter from the moment of denial until the Resurrection? The faces of the disciples would be a reminder of his act. And what were his first thoughts when Mary Magdalene arrived that Sunday morning with news that the body was missing?

Even those with high-horsepower imaginations have trouble understanding what Peter must have felt. We can sympathize but not empathize. Peter was on a road only he could travel, and the road was dark and cold.

Then something happened. We get word of it in two passages of Scripture. First from the Gospel of Luke: "That very hour they got up and returned to Jerusalem. They found the Eleven and those with them gathered together, who said, 'The Lord has certainly been raised, and has appeared to Simon!'" (24:33–34).

And Paul mentioned the event in his letter to the Corinthians:

> For I passed on to you as most important what
> I also received:
> that Christ died for our sins according
> to the Scriptures,
> that He was buried,
> that He was raised on the third day according
> to the Scriptures,
> and that He appeared to Cephas, then to the
> Twelve. (1 Cor. 15:3–5)

When did this happen? To get our bearings we must take in the context. We find out about the third appearance at the end of the fourth appearance.

Two disciples traveling to the town of Emmaus saw Jesus (details are in the next chapter) and spent time with him. Once the appearance was over, the two raced back up the road to the other disciples, ready to spread the exciting news that Jesus was alive and had appeared to them. But their thunder was stolen. Before they could make the big announcement to the disciples and the other followers gathered there, someone said, "The Lord has certainly been raised, and has appeared to Simon!" (Luke 24:34).

That is all the detail we have. Paul mentioned the meeting in the 1 Corinthians passage, but he surrendered no inside information. All we know is that sometime between appearing to the women in the garden near the tomb and joining the two men on the way to Emmaus, Jesus appeared to Peter.

At some point, Peter was alone and the risen Savior appeared to him.

Why the Secrecy?

God has his secrets. Paul described a man who saw "the third heaven." "I know a man in Christ who was caught up into the third heaven 14 years ago. Whether he was in the body or out of the body, I don't know; God knows. I know that this man—whether in the body or out of the body I do not know, God knows—was caught up into paradise. He heard inexpressible words, which a man is not allowed to speak" (2 Cor. 12:2–4).

"Third heaven" is a euphemism for the heaven in which God dwells. The first heaven is where the birds fly, the second where the stars are, and the third is God's habitat.

Scholars debate who this person was. Most believe Paul was referring to himself in the third person so as not to appear boastful. It could be that Paul had a different man in mind. In either case, someone got a special view of heaven. It must have been an amazing sight. Think of all he must have experienced. And what did he experience? We don't know because, "He heard inexpressible words, which a man is not allowed to speak."

"Not allowed to speak." Literally, "unlawful to utter." The man received a divine gag order. He was granted a special privilege. Thanks to Paul, we know about the event but know nothing more. Whoever he was, he was forbidden to reveal what he learned.

John in his revelation saw things he was not allowed to write. The book of Revelation is an account of his spectacular vision, but it isn't the complete record. John saw things he was not allowed to record. "And when the seven thunders spoke, I was about to write. Then I heard a voice from heaven, saying, 'Seal up what the seven thunders said, and do not write it down!'" (Rev. 10:4).

It's human nature to want to know the details. How did Peter respond? What were his first words? Did Peter apologize? What did Jesus say? We're given none of the answers, and we have to respect that privacy. We can assume certain things to be true, but the details will forever be shared by only Jesus and Peter.

The military, in which secrets are common fare, has the phrase "need to know." In a nutshell, an officer might have a top-secret security clearance, but that doesn't entitle him to know everything that is top secret. He is privy only to those things necessary for him to carry out his duties. He is allowed to know only those things he needs to know.

We don't have a need to know what transpired between Peter and his Savior.

Still, Jesus' appearances were not showmanship. Each one had a specific purpose. Peter was the only one of the original disciples who had a one-on-one meeting with Jesus. (Later, Saul, who would become the apostle Paul, had a personal meeting with Jesus on the Damascus road.)

With Jesus, Endings Become Beginnings

No doubt this private meeting was to set things straight, to bring Peter the inner peace shattered in the high priest's courtyard. Words were spoken that were not meant for our ears.

Peter must have worn his guilt like a lead suit. Such failure would leave scars on mind and heart. The years spent with Jesus, the miles traveled, and the sights seen had all become ashes in the heat of fear and denial. And the harshest critic must have been Peter himself.

What Peter considered the end, Jesus saw as the beginning. Even after hearing of the Resurrection from Mary Magdalene and the other women, Peter must have thought the good news still left him holding the messy bag of his public denial. With Jesus, however, endings are the best place to start; failure is the ideal time to reach for success. Someone had to put Peter back on track, and only Jesus could do that.

Here's how I see it. First is the moment. Somewhere, perhaps in the home where Peter was staying, Jesus appeared. It was just the two of them. Peter's mind began to race. What would have gone through your mind? Should he seize Jesus in great joy? Should he fall to his knees as did the women?

Jesus extended his nail-scarred hands, the wounds clearly visible. Perhaps Peter looked down and saw the puncture marks on Christ's feet. Jesus' forehead was a weave of scars—every scar a reminder of what happened, of what Peter could not face.

I then think Jesus moved closer to the fisherman. Peter's emotions of regret and sorrow boiled within him. Every step Jesus took convicted Peter all the more. Soon the big man's shoulders began to shake; tears flowed in streams.

"I . . . I'm . . . I'm sorry," Peter said.

Jesus spoke. "I know."

Then the Carpenter of Nazareth embraced the fisherman

of Galilee. Through the sobs, the repentance, the forgiveness, Peter's ending became his beginning.

A close encounter of the Jesus kind becomes the closest encounter of any kind.

The Closest Encounter

Life is a city we build. Some think of life as a string of events—one following another like pearls on a string. But the past remains with us. Decisions made often follow us; bad decisions dog our steps and haunt our minds. Peter knew this.

Life is a city with streets and structures all built by our decisions. There are beautiful parks and tree-lined lanes. This is what we show others; it is what we want them to see. But like any city, there are dark alleys. In those dismal places we store the things we're ashamed of, things of embarrassment. In emotional crates we hope to store our regrets, doubts, fears, sorrows, and sins.

Those alleys we travel alone and hope no one will ever catch a glimpse of them, but it is there we are most likely to find Jesus waiting for us. He strolls the dark roads, walks our dead ends, hikes through our emotional and spiritual ghettos, and he doesn't feel sullied by them.

Past indiscretions do not disqualify us for his love. We are not an embarrassment to him. Jesus is a hands-on Savior. He doesn't mind getting his hands dirty. He will turn the dismal past into a glorious future.

The lowest, most horrible period in Peter's life took place in the courtyard of the high priest while Jesus endured one of his many trials. A servant girl asked a question, and the fully adult Peter backpedaled in fear. For him, it was the ultimate failure, and a failure it would have remained if Jesus hadn't gone looking for Peter.

Jesus has a private meeting with each of us. Not for others to see. Just you and Jesus. Not for others to discuss. In those moments we want to retreat, to step away from the One we failed, the One we offended.

We say, "I'm sorry."

Jesus replies, "I know."

Chapter 9

On the Road with Jesus

Lee Strobel, formerly a legal affairs journalist who covered many criminal and civil trials, made an interesting observation in his book *The Case for Christ*. He said, "Without question, the amount of testimony and corroboration of Jesus' postresurrection appearances is staggering. To put it into perspective, if you were to call each one of the witnesses to a court of law to be cross-examined for just fifteen minutes each, and you went around the clock without a break, it would take you from breakfast on Monday until dinner on Friday to hear them all. After listening to 129 straight hours of eyewitness testimony, who could possibly walk away unconvinced?"[1]

One of the closest encounters happened on a stretch of road between Jerusalem and Emmaus. While the meeting between Jesus and Peter has almost no information about it, this account is one of the longest and most detailed.

Emmaus was a small town about seven miles from Jerusalem. Its location is now uncertain. Its name means "warm waters," and the historian Josephus described the town as having warm baths good for healing.[2] Two disciples were on a trip. One is named Cleopas ("renowned father"), and the other is unidentified.

We join them on the road.

> Now that same day two of them were on their way to a village called Emmaus, which was about seven miles from Jerusalem. Together they were discussing everything that had taken place. And while they were discussing and arguing, Jesus Himself came near and began to walk along with them. But they were prevented from recognizing Him. Then He asked them, "What is this dispute that you're having with each other as you are walking?" And they stopped [walking and looked] discouraged.
>
> The one named Cleopas answered Him, "Are You the only visitor in Jerusalem who doesn't know the things that happened there in these days?"
>
> "What things?" He asked them.
>
> So they said to Him, "The things concerning Jesus the Nazarene, who was a Prophet powerful in action and speech before God and all the people, and how our chief priests and leaders handed Him over to be sentenced to death, and they crucified Him. But we were hoping that He was the One who was about to redeem Israel. Besides all this, it's the third day since these things hap-

pened. Moreover, some women from our group astounded us. They arrived early at the tomb, and when they didn't find His body, they came and reported that they had seen a vision of angels who said He was alive. Some of those who were with us went to the tomb and found it just as the women had said, but they didn't see Him."

He said to them, "How unwise and slow you are to believe in your hearts all that the prophets have spoken! Didn't the Messiah have to suffer these things and enter into His glory?" Then beginning with Moses and all the Prophets, He interpreted for them the things concerning Himself in all the Scriptures.

They came near the village where they were going, and He gave the impression that He was going farther. But they urged Him: "Stay with us, because it's almost evening, and now the day is almost over." So He went in to stay with them.

It was as He reclined at the table with them that He took the bread, blessed and broke it, and gave it to them. Then their eyes were opened, and they recognized Him, but He disappeared from their sight. So they said to each other, "Weren't our hearts ablaze within us while He was talking with us on the road and explaining the Scriptures to us?" That very hour they got up and returned to Jerusalem. They found the Eleven and those with them gathered together, who said, "The Lord has certainly been raised, and has appeared to Simon!" Then they began to describe what had happened

> on the road and how He was made known to
> them in the breaking of the bread.
> (Luke 24:13–35)

What a tale! It is rich in detail, emotion, and action. It is also one of the most bizarre accounts in the Bible. Watching how Jesus interacted with these men is revealing and encouraging.

Confused, Depressed, and Disappointed

This was an unhappy pair. Their lives had been overturned, and their emotions were raw and near the surface. All their expectations about Jesus had been dashed against a wood cross.

We can sense their depression as they walked along the dirt road that ran from Jerusalem to Emmaus. Only seven miles, a two- to three-hour walk. They passed the time by discussing the horrible events of the last few days. It was Sunday afternoon, and the spring sun lowered itself to the horizon. As the sun set so did their confidence and belief. Who could blame them? The Crucifixion had upended their universe. Their expectations had been shattered with hammer and iron nails.

They were "discussing and arguing" (v. 15). They couldn't help speaking of the cross, the burial, and their fractured hopes. Each step took them closer to their geographical destination and another step away from what they hoped would be. Horrible events and being fed facts they didn't want to swallow left them rudderless ships in a spiritual storm.

Twilight is that time between light and dark. When it comes in the evening, it means darkness is on the way; but when it comes in the morning, it means the sun is rising. These men didn't know which twilight they were in. Was everything over, or was there more to come? So they talked and argued as they walked toward Emmaus.

Understandably, they were disappointed not only in events but in Jesus. They saw him as a powerful, capable preacher and teacher. To them, he was the hope of redemption. In English, the word *hope* carries the idea of wishful thinking laced with uncertainty. We might hope our baseball team goes to the World Series, but we don't consider it a fact yet to happen. Cleopas and his friend had pinned their confidence on the fact that Jesus was the long-awaited Messiah—their version of the Messiah. The murder of Jesus had blown down their fragile belief.

They admitted their confusion about the testimony given by the women. "Some women from our group astounded us. They arrived early at the tomb, and when they didn't find His body, they came and reported that they had seen a vision of angels who said He was alive" (vv. 22–23). What would you do with news like that? Think about what they heard.

They heard the same testimony, but it was too much to believe. They confessed to being "astounded." Other translations use the word *amazed.* The word (*existemi*) means to knock out of place. Today we'd say, "They knocked me off my feet." The women reported their trip to the tomb, the conversation with angels, and word that Jesus was alive. They were confused, and the truth is, we would be too.

Eyes Wide Shut

In the midst of this passionate discussion, Jesus joined them. It seemed that Jesus sneaked up to them. The way the passage is written, he was already walking with them when they noticed that two had become three.

Here the story takes a strange twist. "And while they were discussing and arguing, Jesus Himself came near and began to walk along with them. But they were prevented from recognizing Him" (vv. 15–16). Mary Magdalene had seemed incapable of identifying Jesus at first; here, these two were purposely prevented from recognizing (fully knowing, perceiving) him. An outside force was limiting their ability to recognize the very one they needed. Why?

There was some teaching coming their way. They had, like so many, assumed that Jesus was the Messiah who would free the Jews from their bondage to Rome and usher in a theocratic kingdom. Their disappointment betrayed their misunderstanding of all Jesus taught. Jesus meant to correct them.

Jesus was kind but blunt. First, he described them as "unwise" (v. 25), literally, possessing no understanding. Some translations use the word *foolish,* but that carries more weight than what the text intends. They weren't fools; they were mistaken.

He also referred to them as having hearts slow to believe. Perhaps like us, they had fallen into the trap of "pick and choose" truth—smorgasbord facts. Jesus had many times spoken of his pending death and resurrection, but that didn't fit the theme of the conquering Messiah.

Then the stranger corrected their assumptions. "Didn't

the Messiah have to suffer these things and enter into His glory?" (v. 26). The suffering, torture, trials, crucifixion, death, and burial were necessary. It all had purpose. It was part of the divine plan.

From that concrete statement Jesus began a Bible study like none other. He began with Moses (meaning the books of Moses, the first five books of the Old Testament) and continued through all the Prophets (the remaining books of the Old Testament, especially the major and minor prophets). In other words, Jesus began with Genesis and continued through Malachi, using the prophecies to show that everything that had occurred happened as it should.

Theologians and Bible scholars spend their lives trying to learn what these disciples heard on a seven-mile trip. It was the shortest, most intensive seminary education ever. One could not put a monetary value on what they heard or experienced.

In the House

When they arrived at Emmaus, Jesus "gave the impression that He was going farther" (v. 28). Interesting phrase. The text implies that Jesus wanted them to think he was continuing his journey. The Greek word is used only here. In other Greek literature, the word means to pretend. This left the two disciples with a decision. Evening was close at hand. Should they have allowed this "unknown" teacher to meander off into the dusk or invite him to stay with them?

They chose the latter, and it was the best decision they ever made. They didn't recognize him; but they did recognize the truth, and that revealed their character. They wanted more of the truth . . . and the Truth. In addition, they recognized their own need. Their preconceptions were being corrected, and they wanted more of that. This was theological therapy. These were two great souls.

In the Upper Room hours before his betrayal, Jesus demonstrated that he was the perfect host. He gathered his disciples, washed their feet, taught them of things to come, prayed for them, and instituted the memorial Lord's Supper. Now, at the invitation of Cleopas and his friend, Jesus showed himself the perfect guest.

In the movie business, screenwriters speak of plot points. A plot point is an event in the story that drives the story forward. It is often a pivotal event that compels the hero's next action. This invitation to Jesus was such a dramatic point. Imagine letting him walk on into the darkening twilight.

Ancient customs about the treatment of visitors were very different from ours. For them, hosting was an art form. A guest in the house was a blessing and was to be treated with great honor. So it was here. A meal was served, but Jesus put a twist in this. "It was as He reclined at the table with them that He took the bread, blessed and broke it, and gave it to them" (v. 30).

This detail is easy to overlook. Breaking bread and asking God's blessing on the meal were the responsibility of the host not the guest, yet Jesus took it on himself. It was a simple act, one repeated thousands of times a day, except this particular act had an unexpected result.

"Then their eyes were opened, and they recognized Him, but He disappeared from their sight" (v. 31). As with all the Resurrection appearances, certain details are withheld. What was it about Jesus' words or actions that opened their eyes? Earlier the text said the two were prevented from recognizing Jesus; now the reverse is the case. "Eyes were opened" comes from a verb that means to open fully, completely, as a newborn opens her eyes for the first time. Also, the verb is passive, meaning it was an act done to the two, not something they did to themselves.

There is a familiar formula here: "He took the bread, blessed and broke it, and gave it to them." Three days before, Jesus did something nearly identical during the Last Supper. Although there are some differences in the original language (in the Upper Room, Jesus "gave thanks" for the bread, whereas here he "speaks well" of the food), the concept and image are nearly identical. Could these men have been in the Upper Room with Jesus? Perhaps. If not, maybe they had heard of the events there.

Something else may have tipped them off to Jesus' identity. In blessing and breaking the bread, Cleopas and his companion must have seen the nail scars in Jesus' hands. It sends shivers down the spine just to imagine the shock of the revelation. Jesus the resurrected sat at their table.

They recognized (*epegnosan*) him—knew him fully; they understood completely. After a seven-mile journey from Jerusalem to Emmaus during which a stranger taught and corrected them, a trek that began with them submerged in the deepest despair, the two suddenly understood.

Then Jesus disappeared. Before their now open eyes, Jesus simply ceased to be there. That must have set their hearts tumbling. They were still holding bread given to them by someone who had vanished in a moment.

Reentry

The appearance changed them in profound ways. They went from disheartened disciples to dynamos. The two who had left Jerusalem depressed made a decision to rush back up the seven-mile road, even though the sun was down. Lit by a waning full moon, the two left their home and raced along the path they had just traveled. Understanding prompts action. They had a story to tell, and neither distance nor weariness was going to keep them from sharing all that they had seen and heard.

One of the most interesting aspects of this passage is the reason they gave for their excitement: "So they said to each other, 'Weren't our hearts ablaze within us while He was talking with us on the road and explaining the Scriptures to us?'" (v. 32).

Not the sudden appearance of the stranger, not the way he took the hosting responsibility, not the way he looked or the bizarre disappearance, but the unveiling of scriptural truth set their hearts ablaze. Very few people could claim to have seen what they did, but they were most moved by knowing that Jesus was meant to suffer, die, be buried, and then resurrected. It is that understanding that put their feet on the road again.

Perhaps this is where the lesson is for us. Seeing may be believing, but understanding is better. Later, Jesus told Thomas, "Because you have seen Me, you have believed. Those who believe without seeing are blessed" (John 20:29). When the Scriptures were opened to these men, they came to understand the big picture. In some ways, we understand more than they did. We have four Gospel accounts and many other New Testament books to shed light on the great mysteries of God. The Old Testament is revealed through the New Testament. We have sixty-six books of inspired text to guide our thinking. While we may not have seen Jesus in the flesh, we have the truth of his nature and work.

Perhaps the most moving element of this account is how Jesus took the time to join them. They were disheartened and depressed until he entered the picture. And how did Jesus meet their need? With a soft-spoken, "There, there now; things will get better" and a pat on the back? No. Jesus aimed at the mind first. Their hearts followed their understanding. Jesus explained; they listened and were changed. Two thousand years later, the same is true.

I've often wondered why their eyes were prevented from seeing. It occurs to me now that they, like us, need groundwork. Before a landscape architect does his work, he analyzes the land, the building, the soil, and the needs of his client. Only then can he create a plan that will work. Perhaps Jesus does the same with us. Information is more valuable when we have it at the right time and use it for the right need.

The two disciples were not ready to see Jesus. They were "unwise and slow" to believe. They were lost in a storm of preconceived ideas and mounting waves of disappointment. Only after they had the biblical basis for Christ's death and resurrection could they see and believe.

Their hearts beat faster with the truth of Scripture in their minds. So will ours.

The greatest danger to the church today is ignorance. In an entertainment-driven society, Bible knowledge has become as thin as tissue paper. When Jesus dealt with these two, he aimed first at the mind. The emotion would follow.

There is much talk in churches about giving our hearts to Christ. No crime there, but to give the heart we must also give the mind.

For Cleopas and friend, Jesus was the rabbi on the road, and it was knowledge that made their hearts burn within them.

Chapter 10

The Unexpected Guest

They were in a dim and stuffy room. Outside the sun had set beyond the hills; the spring day was cooling rapidly. They could hear noises from the streets—sounds of the thousands who had come to Jerusalem to celebrate Passover just a few days before. Now other feast days were before them.

The darkness outside matched the darkness inside. A group of men assembled. It was the room over Mark's house, the room where Jesus broke bread and poured out wine.[1]

They were a gathering of men too ashamed to go home, too frightened to walk the streets, too embarrassed to face others. These were the men called disciples—three-year travelers with Jesus. They walked the land, following the Carpenter of Nazareth, from Galilee in the north, through the despised Samaria, and throughout Judea in the south.

These were men who not only had witnessed miracles but performed them when empowered by Jesus. Outcasts like Matthew the tax collector, big men like Peter the fisherman, sensitive men like John.

All but one had proven himself a coward.

Strange things had been happening; weird encounters were spoken of with excitement. Even Peter had encountered the risen Christ. Now, two disciples, Cleopas and the unnamed one, were perched on their toes ready to pour out their encounter when it happened.

Through locked doors came Jesus—and everything changed.

Seeing the risen Jesus could be exhilarating—it could also be terrifying. In some of Jesus' postresurrection appearances, he defied the laws of biology and physics. Usually, seeing is believing; but with such extraordinary events, our minds can refuse to believe our eyes. Notice what such an unexpected appearance did to the disciples.

> And as they were saying these things, He Himself stood among them. He said to them, "Peace to you!" But they were startled and terrified and thought they were seeing a ghost. "Why are you troubled?" He asked them. "And why do doubts arise in your hearts? Look at My hands and My feet, that it is I Myself! Touch Me and see, because a ghost does not have flesh and bones as you can see I have." Having said this, He showed them His hands and feet. But while they still could not believe because of their joy and were amazed, He asked them, "Do you have anything here to eat?" So they gave Him a piece of a broiled fish, and He took it and ate in their presence.

> Then He told them, "These are My words that I spoke to you while I was still with you—that everything written about Me in the Law of Moses, the Prophets, and the Psalms must be fulfilled." Then He opened their minds to understand the Scriptures. He also said to them, "This is what is written: the Messiah would suffer and rise from the dead the third day, and repentance for forgiveness of sins would be proclaimed in His name to all the nations, beginning at Jerusalem. You are witnesses of these things. And look, I am sending you what My Father promised. As for you, stay in the city until you are empowered from on high." (Luke 24:36–49)

The Unexpected Jesus

The huddle of frightened men became all the more frightened. Cleopas and friend have just arrived after their return trip from Emmaus. They expected to dazzle the disciples with their account of how Jesus joined them on the road, corrected their thinking with a seven-mile Bible study, came into their home, broke bread, then disappeared, when the others sprang the news that Peter had had a visit from Jesus as well.

The story was barely out when Jesus joined them—in a most unusual way (Luke 24:36–38). Jesus came when they least expected it and in a fashion no one could predict. He walked through solid matter. "In the evening of that first day of the week, the disciples were [gathered together] with the doors locked because of their fear of the Jews. Then Jesus came, stood among them, and said to them, 'Peace to you!'" (John 20:19).

Locked doors were no problem for Jesus. Here was one of the most interesting aspects of Jesus' resurrection. He made a point (as we will see) of proving that he was physically raised—not a ghost, a mirage, or an illusion—that his body in the Resurrection was as real as before his death. Yet, he appeared and disappeared as he wished, and at times it seemed he did so to make a point.

Jesus came to them. It's an important distinction. So far, Jesus had taken the initiative. He appeared to Mary and the other women in the garden, to Peter in an undisclosed place, to the two disciples on the way to Emmaus, and now to a room filled with frightened people. In every case we've seen so far, and in every case we shall see, Jesus chose to whom he made himself known. No one ever stumbled on the resurrected Jesus. During his ministry, people often sought him out. They traveled to listen to his voice, perchance to be touched by his hands. After the Resurrection, that changed.

Peter alluded to this in a message he gave: "'God raised up this man [Jesus] on the third day and permitted Him to be seen, not by all the people, but by us, witnesses appointed beforehand by God, who ate and drank with Him after He rose from the dead'" (Acts 10:40–41).

It was this moment and a later one that Peter was recalling. Jesus was selective. He appeared, as far as the biblical record shows, only to select persons. Jesus sought out those who would be witnesses to his resurrection. It was no accident that everyone who saw Jesus felt compelled immediately to tell others.

This is the largest group he appeared to, so far, and these people were far from the mighty men of God they would become and the way we usually think of them. They were frightened people, huddled in a dim room and fearing for their lives. The people who orchestrated Jesus' death were still in the city, and most could recognize the disciples on sight.

At first Jesus' appearance only added to their trauma.

More Shocking Than They Guessed

Flabbergasted. Stunned. Shocked. Staggered. Amazed. Bowled over. A dozen other words could be used to describe the emotional storm raging in each of them.

Note the different words used to describe their emotional state. First, they were startled (v. 37). A more literal rendering is alarmed (*ptothentes*). Seeing a man walk into a closed room was unsettling. Hearts began to race.

They were also terrified (*emphoboi*). The word describes fright in response to, in this case, something seen. First, shocking terror mixed with abiding fear.

Although not stated, one more emotion is implied: confusion—"thought they were seeing a ghost" (v. 37). It was a natural thought. Jesus had just walked through a wall or locked door.

Those three emotions are given from the disciples' point of view. Jesus used two terms that help us understand the psychology of the moment. "Why are you troubled?" he asked them. "And why do doubts arise in your hearts?" (v. 38).

Jesus saw two more emotions, and he called them to their attention. He asked why they were troubled (*tetaragmenoi*), agitated, stirred up. They were like a pot of boiling water—emotions out of control. Then he asked about their doubts. Actually, he questioned their reasoning. Wuest's translation has Jesus question this way: "Wherefore do reasonings come up in your hearts?"[2] In other words, the disciples could not believe their eyes. Their unspoken conclusion was that a ghost had joined them.

Very few people would be so arrogant as to blame them. I would have responded in the same fashion. Frankly, I can't think of anyone who wouldn't.

The irony of this is that Jesus appeared and wished them peace. They felt everything but peace.

Beyond Imagination

We have only our imaginations to help us see how Jesus came into the room. Did he just materialize? Did the disciples see him pass through the door or wall? No one can say. We do know that the appearance was enough to upset the group including Peter, Cleopas, and the unnamed Emmaus disciple.

A hint comes from the unspoken assumption: They "thought they were seeing a ghost" (v. 37b). Jesus knew their thoughts and responded: "'Look at My hands and My feet, that it is I Myself! Touch Me and see, because a ghost does not have flesh and bones as you can see I have.' Having said this, He showed them His hands and feet" (vv. 39–40).

To dispel their fear and correct their erroneous conclusion, Jesus offered two forms of evidence. He commanded them to look at his hands and feet. More and more, our world is using biometrics to identify individuals. Fingerprints are the most common biometric. Every person has a fingerprint pattern unique to him. It cannot be altered or duplicated. The fingerprints of a criminal at a crime scene are enough to put him in jail. New biometrics include retina scans and devices that recognize the blood vein pattern on the back of a person's hand. Interesting, isn't it? Jesus' biometric identification was the wounds from his crucifixion.

But he encouraged them to do more than merely look. Jesus challenged them to touch him. The command was to handle him, to grope in the sense of a blind man fingering something to determine what it is. They were to look and touch. It would require courage, but it would forever change their lives.

How important an invitation was this? One of the men there, John, would later write:

> What was from the beginning,
> what we have heard,
> what we have seen with our eyes,
> what we have observed,
> and have touched with our hands,
> concerning the Word of life—
> (1 John 1:1)

John may have had this moment in mind when he penned those words.

Jesus emphasized the physical. In the decades that followed this appearance, groups like the Gnostics would do their best to convince believers that Jesus' resurrection was not physical but spiritual. Twenty centuries later, certain groups advocate the same nonsense. Jesus went out of his way to appear physically and to make certain his followers knew he was not mere spirit but flesh and bones.

Slowly, tentatively, the disciples did as commanded; and once they did, they came to know that the Resurrection was a fact, not a fable. How personal and intimate an invitation Jesus made. He wanted to dispel their fear and fill that void with the joy of truth.

More Emotion Than They Could Handle

If we had been in that room, we would have been awash in the same tide of emotion. I have no problem seeing those grown men in tears of joy. Of course, they were conflicted. Who wouldn't be?

Good news can be as stunning as bad news. Shock is shock no matter what its origins. This band of brothers went from fear to joy to amazement. In some ways, they were overjoyed. I've always thought that is an odd word. *Overjoyed.* Can a person be too happy? Be filled with too much joy? It happens. Every year the Publishers Clearing House Sweepstakes awards someone a great deal of money. The winner comes to the door and more often than not screams, "I don't believe it!" Her behavior, however—the dancing, shouting, tears—indicates otherwise. She believes it but can't believe it. It seems a contradiction, but it is still true. The disciples must have felt the same way.

They were also amazed. A good synonym would be mind-boggled. Facing the incredible and realizing it is credible can cause a mental meltdown. Jesus took one more step to prove he was corporeal and not imaginary. He asked for food. "But while they still could not believe because of their joy and were amazed, He asked them, 'Do you have anything here to eat?' So they gave Him a piece of a broiled fish, and He took it and ate in their presence" (vv. 41–43).

Since ghosts don't eat, Jesus took the offered fish and "ate in their presence." He ate not because he was hungry but because it was one more piece of evidence for the disciples.

Almost as amazing as Jesus' sudden appearance (and unique way of arriving on the scene) was his accommodating nature. He didn't challenge the disciples or criticize them for their confusion. Instead, he went the distance to ease their minds and prove his physical resurrection.

Insight

> Then He told them, "These are My words that I spoke to you while I was still with you—that everything written about Me in the Law of Moses, the Prophets, and the Psalms must be fulfilled." Then He opened their minds to understand the Scriptures. He also said to them, "This is what is written: the Messiah would suffer and rise from the dead the third day, and repentance for forgiveness of sins would be proclaimed in His name to all the nations, beginning at Jerusalem. You are witnesses of these things. And look, I am sending you what My Father promised. As for you, stay in the city until you are empowered from on high." (Luke 24:44–49)

Once the disciples could believe their eyes, ears, and hands, they were ready for the reason Jesus came to visit.

First, he used a phrase that is easy to skip over—or trip over: "while I was still with you." After going to lengths to prove he was just as real and physical as everyone else in the room, Jesus now separated himself. He had been changed. Things were not going back to the way they were. His teaching ministry was not going to pick up on Sunday where it left off the previous Thursday. For three years he was with them on a daily basis. They rose every morning and knew Jesus would be there. Not now. Not anymore. Jesus would no longer be the itinerate preacher. Instead, he was going to be the risen and ascended Savior.

During his earthly ministry Jesus taught his disciples that centuries of anticipation recorded in the Law of Moses, the Prophets, and the Psalms had been fulfilled in him. Jesus used the threefold division of the Old Testament common in the first century. Sometimes a twofold division was used: the Law and Prophets. The point Jesus made was the whole Old Testament points to him.

"Then He opened their minds to understand the Scriptures" (v. 45). The two Emmaus disciples had already had their eyes opened to recognize Jesus, and now everyone in the room received a gift of supernaturally guided understanding. The implication is that their minds had been closed to the biblical evidence.

They needed help, and Jesus provided it. No details are given about what Jesus actually did to open their minds to the Scriptures, but it was certainly an "Aha!" moment.

Then came the brief but life-altering lesson. From the beginning, Jesus taught, it was meant for the Messiah to come, suffer, die, and be resurrected on the third day. He added that repentance for the forgiveness of sins would be proclaimed throughout the world, beginning in Jerusalem. Acts 2 is the record of that first proclamation. It didn't take much eye opening for the disciples to understand they would be the message bearers.

The word translated witness (*martures*) is the word for martyr. Of the remaining eleven disciples only one, John, would die a natural death but only after years of persecution and banishment. In many ways he was a martyr too.

Those were the future facts, and they came with a future promise: "I am sending you what my Father promised" (v. 49). Although not stated here, we know that Jesus was referring to the Holy Spirit who descended on the disciples about fifty days from that moment. They were to stay in the city until "empowered from on high," literally, clothed in power, might, and force. For the moment, their job was to wait.

Influence

Moments before, they had been a congregation of the timid, of the frightened, cloistered behind locked doors, trying to make sense of what they had heard from the women, Peter, and now Cleopas and friend.

Then Jesus reentered their lives. Not a battered, tortured man but the risen Savior—altered in indescribable ways but still a very physical Jesus.

Now they knew. The cross was not an end but a beginning. All they had lived for, sacrificed for, would continue, and they were chosen to carry on the task.

They didn't know what lay before them. Which one of us knows what Jesus has around the corner for us? We can plan, prepare, and dream, but the future remains unformed in our minds.

It is good to know that our search for spiritual understanding is never done alone, but that Jesus opens the minds of believers to understand and apply the Scriptures.

It is a great legacy we carry—one begun in a dark room among a group of the least likely heroes. Out of the timid, Jesus made witnesses who turned the world upside down.

And it began with an unexpected visitor.

Chapter 11

The Odd Man Out

In June 1975, then-President Gerald Ford arrived at Salzburg, Austria. As usual the fanfare that accompanies the arrival of a head of state greeted him. He stepped from Air Force One, waved at the crowd, and started down the steps from the jet toward the tarmac. As he reached the last few steps, he stumbled, falling to the ground. Embarrassed, he sprang to his feet and brushed himself off. According to his autobiography *A Time to Heal,* he gave it no further thought. Unfortunately for him, others were not so willing to let the slip . . . slip.

Comedians Johnny Carson and Chevy Chase milked the mishap for all it was worth. Soon Ford had the image of an unsteady klutz prone to falls and missteps. This image haunts him to this day. Ford wrote about Carson's and Chase's portrayals of him, "Their antics—and I'll admit that I laughed at them myself—helped create the public perception of me as a stumbler. And that wasn't funny."[1]

Here's the irony. Gerald Ford was an athlete. He played college football and loved to ski, something he continued through his presidential years. The image of him as unsteady on his feet couldn't have been more wrong. Still, the image remains.

The New Testament equivalent of such unjust and inaccurate labeling is the disciple Thomas. Thomas got a bad rap. In truth, he may represent most of us more than any other disciple does—at least in this case. Thomas had missed a few things. That may have been bad for him, but it has been good for us.

> But one of the Twelve, Thomas (called "Twin"), was not with them when Jesus came. So the other disciples kept telling him, "We have seen the Lord!"
>
> But he said to them, "If I don't see the mark of the nails in His hands, put my finger into the mark of the nails, and put my hand into His side, I will never believe!"
>
> After eight days His disciples were indoors again, and Thomas was with them. Even though the doors were locked, Jesus came and stood among them. He said, "Peace to you!"
>
> Then He said to Thomas, "Put your finger here and observe My hands. Reach out your hand and put it into My side. Don't be an unbeliever, but a believer."
>
> Thomas responded to Him, "My Lord and my God!"
>
> Jesus said, "Because you have seen Me, you have believed. Those who believe without seeing are blessed." (John 20:24–29)

Thomas has been carrying the title "doubter" for two thousand years. Perhaps because this is the most we see of Thomas in the biblical record and therefore assume that this single act defined him as a man. But there was more to Thomas than most know.

Thomas appears three other times in the Gospel of John. Except for the listing of the disciples, Thomas does not appear in the other three Gospels. He was a background player, but that doesn't make him insignificant.

Usually referred to as "doubting Thomas," he was the most misrepresented disciple. I think he deserves a better tag line. We could call him Thomas the courageous.

When Lazarus died in the tiny town of Bethany, Jesus told his disciples he was going there (John 11:7). That didn't sit well with the men: "Rabbi, . . . just now the Jews tried to stone You, and You're going there again?" (John 11:8). They had a right to be concerned. A physical attack on Jesus could easily have become an attack on them. Stoning was a horrible way to die. It involved dropping the condemned into a wide pit and then pummeling him with various-sized stones until he was dead. The danger was real, but their fears did not alter Jesus' plan.

Now they had a decision to make. To go with Jesus or to wait for him to return. Thomas broke the silence: "Then Thomas (called 'Twin') said to his fellow disciples, 'Let's go so that we may die with Him'" (John 11:16). He didn't say, "Let's go so we can protect him." Thomas assumed Jesus was on a suicide mission and chose to join him in it. It took unusual courage to march toward one's own death. As it turned out, no stoning took place, but Thomas didn't know that beforehand.

The disciple was not only courageous, he also possessed a keen spiritual curiosity.

Sandwiched between two of the most famous verses in the Bible is a little question that reveals a great deal about the disciple named Thomas. We often hear John 14:1–4 at funerals. Its mention of mansions/dwelling places prepared by Jesus in his "Father's house" paints a comforting image. "'Your heart must not be troubled. Believe in God; believe also in Me. In My Father's house are many dwelling places; if not, I would have told you. I am going away to prepare a place for you. If I go away and prepare a place for you, I will come back and receive you to Myself, so that where I am you may be also. You know the way where I am going.'"

John 14:6 is often used in evangelism and in the defense of Christ as the only means of salvation: "Jesus told him, 'I am the way, the truth, and the life. No one comes to the Father except through Me.'" It is a powerful verse as are those that precede it. Perhaps it is because these verses radiate so much imagery and information that the short verse 5 is so often overlooked: "'Lord,' Thomas said, 'we don't know where You're going. How can we know the way?'"

These were the words of a confused man, a man willing to acknowledge his ignorance and display his desire to know. There was a spiritual hunger. Just as Thomas was willing to return with Jesus to Judea even though it might have meant a painful death, he was willing to go with Jesus to a place he didn't understand. What makes this so refreshing was his uncomplicated desire to know what Jesus was teaching. There was no pretense about the man. He said what he thought even if it meant admitting he was lagging behind on the learning curve. To be so honest with oneself is rare.

Courageous, honest, self-aware, Thomas deserves a better title than "doubter." Still, when confronted by the testimony of his fellow disciples, Thomas wanted more.

The Three I's of Thomas

Jesus walked into a locked room in full view of the gathered disciples. He went out of his way to prove he was no ghost but flesh and bone. Everyone saw it and heard it—everyone except Thomas. He missed the whole thing.

We have no idea where Thomas was when Jesus appeared to the others in the room. It's futile to guess. He might have needed time alone, been praying, visiting with someone, or just hiding out in a different part of the city. Wherever he was, whatever he was doing, he missed something grand.

It is part of human nature for those who have experienced something wonderful and life changing to immediately want to share it with others.

Thomas was the other.

No sooner had he made his way to the meeting spot of the disciples than he was hammered with the news. "So the other disciples kept telling him, 'We have seen the Lord!'" (John 20:25a). The way this is worded indicates that Thomas's friends not only told him this, they kept telling him, and telling him, and telling him. Perhaps this is why Thomas's response comes across so terse.

Thomas replied, "If I don't see the mark of the nails in His hands, put my finger into the mark of the nails, and put my hand into His side, I will never believe!" (v. 25b).

There it is—the statement that has stained Thomas's image for two thousand years. In those few words, Thomas lays out his three I's: "If *I* don't see, if *I* don't touch, then *I* will not believe."

The disciples repeatedly argued, "We have seen the Lord." But that wasn't enough for Thomas. Not by a long shot. Just days before, in a matter of hours, Thomas's world had been upended. Now, three days later, his friends are making a statement he couldn't swallow.

When "We" Doesn't Mean "Me"

Thomas was a skeptic but not a fool. Michael Shermer has a unique job. He's a professional skeptic. He is the founder of *Skeptic* magazine and the author of *The Borderlands of Science* and other books. Each month he writes an article for the prestigious magazine *Scientific American.* He gets paid to write about why everyone else's beliefs are wrong. For me, especially when he writes about matters of faith, his logic falters. At times, it seems skeptics like Dr. Shermer are in love with skepticism more than truth.

Still, people like Shermer do us a favor. They force us to think, to question, to seek deeper answers when we've been comfortable merely looking at the surface.

It wasn't that Thomas didn't believe but that he withheld his belief. He was the pragmatist. He had seen miracles and, imbued with power from Christ, performed miracles during those times when Jesus sent the disciples out teaching and preaching (see Luke 9:1–2). Thomas didn't have a problem with the spiritual, but his friends were asking him to believe the difficult. His desire for proof wasn't rooted in obstinacy but in respect for his Lord.

One of the great Christian myths is that faith is belief

in the absence of evidence. We have phrases such as "Take it on faith" and "I can't prove it to you, you'll just have to have faith." The Bible never defines faith that way. In fact, the biblical definition is the opposite. In what is one of the few cases in which the Bible defines one of its own terms, the writer of Hebrews describes faith this way: "Now faith is the reality of what is hoped for, the proof of what is not seen" (11:1).

Reality and *proof* are two concrete words. Faith is a reasoned belief, not a wild leap in the dark. This is especially true when it comes to Christ's resurrection. Luke started his book of Acts by writing, "After He had suffered, He also presented Himself alive to them by many convincing proofs, appearing to them during 40 days and speaking about the kingdom of God" (1:3). Jesus demonstrated the truth of his resurrection by presenting "convincing proofs."

Considering Thomas's relationship to Jesus and his understanding of the other disciples, we conclude he was within his rights to want more evidence.

Many religions provide good feelings. The whole New Age movement centers on that. If the goal is simply to "feel good," Christianity isn't a good choice. There are less demanding belief systems. If being in fellowship with God is the goal, Christianity is the only choice.

Thomas reminded us of something else: We all come to Jesus one on one. At a Billy Graham crusade, thousands may walk to the front to receive Christ, but every one of those decisions is one person connecting to the Savior. Thomas was no different. He would have to come to belief in his own way.

The Lull Between Storms

One of the most amazing aspects of this account is the time element. Eight days went by before Jesus appeared to the group again. "After eight days His disciples were indoors again, and Thomas was with them. Even though the doors were locked, Jesus came and stood among them. He said, 'Peace to you!'" (John 20:26).

In some ways, this was the week that wasn't. We have no idea what Thomas did that week. We don't know where Jesus was or what he did during that time. Eight days passed with no information. The only thing we can glean from the passages is that the disciples were still in hiding or at least meeting in secret. We know this because the passage tells us the doors were locked.

The dynamics of the group had changed. For the male disciples, those who had been closest to Jesus went from one who had seen (Peter) and ten who hadn't to ten who had and one who hadn't (Thomas). They were still friends, comrades in a great calling; but for a solid week, Thomas was the odd man out.

Questions buzzed around this week like bees around a hive. Did Thomas rationalize for eight days? *The others have been under a lot of stress.* Did he agonize for that week? Did he fear he had missed his chance? Eight days of wondering, guessing, internal debating. Insider became an outsider. The others had experienced something he hadn't.

Challenged faith is a strong faith. Thomas was willing to ask, "How?" He was keen to say, "Let's go die." He was ready to listen. He was willing to doubt what he heard. "I need more." And he was willing to look for it.

The key is, he was willing to be convinced. He did not doubt because he preferred doubt. He didn't question what the others had seen because he enjoyed being the naysayer. He hungered for the truth and wanted to believe.

No amount of evidence will convince a man who is comfortable in his disbelief, and Thomas was anything but comfortable.

That discomfort turned hot when Jesus appeared in the closed room.

The Jesus Challenge

There are several shockers in this passage, not the least of which are Jesus' words. He began with the typical "Peace be with you" but then turned his eyes on one person. The silence must have been palpable. "Then He said to Thomas, 'Put your finger here and observe My hands. Reach out your hand and put it into My side. Don't be an unbeliever, but a believer.' Thomas responded to Him, 'My Lord and my God!'" (John 20:27–28).

Jesus knew what had been said behind closed doors, and he was calling Thomas on it. The words came with a series of commands: put, observe, reach, and believe. Every one an intimate order. Some of the commands were chilling: "Finger the nail marks in my hands. Stick your hand in the wound in my side." The extent Jesus went to make Thomas see and believe was amazing. It also reminds us Jesus still has his wounds.

It's one thing to demand proof, but another thing to follow through. Thomas saw and heard Jesus. Christ was acquiescing to Thomas's demand, and suddenly Thomas has no taste for it. He didn't reach, didn't touch, but he did believe, and that belief drove him to his knees in worship.

Firm demands melt in the presence of Jesus. "My Lord and my God!" It says it all. In Jewish context this is blasphemy, but Thomas could state only what he knew to be true, and Jesus allowed it. He did not correct Thomas, because what Thomas had admitted was true and proper. That can be said only of Jesus.

Some people tried to perform the same homage to Peter, but he refused it. "When Peter entered, Cornelius met him, fell at his feet, and worshiped him. But Peter helped him up and said, 'Stand up! I myself am also a man'" (Acts 10:25–26).

Unlike Peter, Jesus didn't object. In fact, no one objected. The only explanation for this is that they all agreed with Thomas.

The Open Invitation

For many, seeing is believing. That was true for Thomas, and Jesus acknowledged it; but he added something meant for those not in the room, for those who would not have the opportunity to see Jesus in the flesh, at least in this life: "Jesus said, 'Because you have seen Me, you have believed. Those who believe without seeing are blessed'" (John 20:29).

There is no doubt that Thomas was blessed to have seen Jesus in his resurrected form, but the blessing didn't end with Jesus' ascension to heaven nearly forty days later. At that moment, Jesus was focused on Thomas, but he also had his eye on us. Jesus added a simple phrase that touches every believer to come: "Those who believe without seeing are blessed."

Blessed means to be made happy or to be considered fortunate. Jesus was not merely describing the blessed state of future believers, he was at that moment blessing them and blessing us. So powerful a statement is this that Peter decades later included it in his first letter: "You love Him, though you have not seen Him. And though not seeing Him now, you believe in Him and rejoice with inexpressible and glorious joy, because you are receiving the goal of your faith, the salvation of your souls" (1 Pet. 1:8–9).

Edwin Blum said, "Believers living today are not deprived by not seeing Him physically; instead, they are the recipients of His special blessing."[2]

Every Christian would love to see Jesus in the flesh as Thomas did. The impact of such a meeting would be burned into every brain cell. Because of that, we assume that those who saw Jesus in the flesh are blessed more than we who stand twenty centuries later. No one can argue that seeing Jesus was a secondary, lesser blessing, but it would be just as erroneous to claim that believers who came later are any less blessed. Jesus does more than call us blessed who have not seen him in the flesh yet believe; he does the blessing himself.

Thomas had an opportunity to represent those who believe without seeing, but he insisted on having the same experience as Mary, the women, and the disciples.

Perhaps this is where those who so fiercely attack the fact of the Resurrection err. Empirical evidence is not always proof that leads to belief. The religious leaders who opposed Jesus saw miracles, heard his teaching, knew the scriptural prophecies and more, yet they made the conscious choice to not only disbelieve but to oppose all the Savior did.

In Luke 16:19–31, Jesus related the story of two men. Often called a parable, this account is not fiction told to teach, it is the unveiling of a real event. (If it is a parable, it is the only one in which Jesus used a proper name.)

The rich man and Lazarus were at the center of the account. This was not the same Lazarus as Jesus' friend from Bethany whom he raised back to life. The rich man was described, but no name was given. Tradition calls him Dives, which, while impossible to prove, serves as a useful handle.

It is a story of contrasts. The rich man had everything a person of his time could want; Lazarus had nothing but the pity of others. The two had one thing in common: They were mortal. Both died but opened their eyes in very different circumstances.

Lazarus rested in a place of comfort and peace, consoled by the father of the Jews, Abraham. Dives didn't fare so well. He awoke in the torment of Hades. A dialogue between Dives and Abraham ensued.

> "Father Abraham!" he called out, "Have mercy on me and send Lazarus to dip the tip of his finger in water and cool my tongue, because I am in agony in this flame!"
>
> "Son," Abraham said, "remember that during your life you received your good things, just as Lazarus received bad things, but now he is comforted here, while you are in agony. Besides all this, a great chasm has been fixed between us and you, so that those who want to pass over from here to you cannot; neither can those from there cross over to us."

> "Father," he said, "then I beg you to send him to my father's house—because I have five brothers—to warn them, so they won't also come to this place of torment."
>
> But Abraham said, "They have Moses and the prophets; they should listen to them."
>
> "No, father Abraham," he said. "But if someone from the dead goes to them, they will repent."
>
> But he told him, "If they don't listen to Moses and the prophets, they will not be persuaded if someone rises from the dead." (Luke 16:24–31)

The last two verses are revealing. Dives was under the impression that someone, like Lazarus, returning from the dead would be all the proof anyone needed to come to faith. Abraham knew better. Even if Lazarus was returned to life, it would make no difference to those who chose not to believe.

Jesus never appeared to his enemies, preferring to reveal himself to those who had the heart and mind to believe. Belief is a rational decision that begins in the mind and then changes the heart. Thomas was not an unbeliever; he was a person of faith who in a time of the highest confusion longed to see what others had. His faith would have been no less powerful had Jesus not arrived on the scene eight days later.

It is that time frame that again proves a point. After a week of hearing the others speak of Jesus' sighting, he remained with them. The days clicked by like hours on the clock, and still Thomas was found with his friends and fellow believers. Jesus did not have to go looking for him. He knew Thomas would be with the other disciples. Thomas was held by a bond of common experience and faith that sealed him to the others.

Harry Houdini made a name for himself by escaping from every imaginable confinement—from straitjackets to multiple pairs of handcuffs clamped to his arms. He boasted that no jail cell could hold him. Time and time again, he would be locked in a cell only to reappear minutes later.

It worked every time—but one.

He accepted another invitation to demonstrate his skill. He entered the cell, wearing his street clothes, and the jail cell door shut. Once alone, he pulled a thin but strong piece of metal from his belt and began working the lock. But something was wrong. No matter how hard Houdini worked, he couldn't unlock the lock. For two hours he applied skill and experience to the lock but failed time and time again. Two hours later he gave up in frustration.

The problem? The cell had never been locked. Houdini worked himself to near exhaustion trying to achieve what could be accomplished by simply pushing the door open. The only place the door was locked was in his mind.

Faith is not a complex process. It is not the result of years of education, pilgrimages, or flashy supernatural experience. The door to belief is ready to open and is locked only in the minds of those who choose to believe it is.

Chapter 12

Mountaintop Experience

It is common for people to speak of a mountaintop experience. Some of my most memorable experiences have happened on mountaintops. Each year hundreds of pastors from California gather at Hume Lake for such a time. There are worship services, conferences, music, and Bible studies . . . and fishing tournaments, golf matches, sports, horseback riding, and other highly ministerial activities.

For most, it's a time of refreshment and relaxation. It is also an opportunity to become reacquainted with the Lord. The problem with mountaintop experiences is that, sooner or later, you have to drive back to the valley.

Two thousand years ago about 511 people had a close encounter of the Jesus kind on a mountain in Galilee. It changed them forever. It changed the world.

> The 11 disciples traveled to Galilee, to the mountain where Jesus had directed them. When

they saw Him, they worshiped, but some doubted. Then Jesus came near and said to them, "All authority has been given to Me in heaven and on earth. Go, therefore, and make disciples of all nations, baptizing them in the name of the Father and of the Son and of the Holy Spirit, teaching them to observe everything I have commanded you. And remember, I am with you always, to the end of the age." (Matt. 28:16–20)

Then He appeared to over 500 brothers
at one time,
most of whom remain to the present,
but some have fallen asleep. (1 Cor. 15:6)

Five Hundred Eleven Close Friends

One of the most difficult tasks facing the Bible student is placing the Resurrection appearances in their "proper" order. I place *proper* in quotes for a reason. Western world thinkers are used to placing things and events in linear order. A follows B, which leads to C. For most of us it is difficult to think in any other way. But the ancient Middle Eastern mind followed a different set of rules. Events were more important than the time they occurred. This is why the order of events in the Gospels does not line up. They were never intended to. Each author followed an outline that best served his purpose, emphasizing certain actions over others.

With the Resurrection appearances we have to make some assumptions. For example, here I assume that the appearance of Christ to the five hundred occurred at the same time as his appearance to the eleven in Galilee.

There are several reasons to assume this. One, the appearance occurred outside of Jerusalem. Jesus met with his followers in Galilee in the northern part of the country. In several appearances, Jesus sent word that his disciples were to meet him in Galilee, but we know the earliest manifestations were in or around Jerusalem.

Also, the Galilee area was home to many of his followers, not only the eleven closest but hundreds of others who followed his early ministry. This was home to the disciples. Only Judas Iscariot was from someplace other than Galilee.

They came to this place by command.

> From Jesus to the disciples: "Tonight all of you will run away because of Me, for it is written: I will strike the shepherd, and the sheep of the flock will be scattered. But after I have been resurrected, *I will go ahead of you to Galilee.*" (Matt. 26:31–32)
>
> From the angel to the women at the tomb: "Don't be afraid, because I know you are looking for Jesus who was crucified. He is not here! For He has been resurrected, just as He said. Come and see the place where He lay. Then go quickly and tell His disciples, 'He has been raised from the dead. In fact, *He is going ahead of you to Galilee; you will see Him there.*' Listen, I have told you." (Matt. 28:5–7)
>
> From Jesus to the women at the tomb: "Do not be afraid. *Go and tell My brothers to leave for Galilee, and they will see Me there.*" (Matt. 28:10)

During one of the Jerusalem encounters and before his death, Jesus had indicated a particular mountain. The Bible doesn't tell us which mountain.

The second group of people there are simply referred to as the five hundred (1 Cor. 15:6). Usually groups numbered only the men,[1] so the number could be larger if there were women present, and there's no reason to believe that Mary Magdalene and many others were not present. Whatever the actual number, Paul referred to them as the five hundred brethren. He went so far as to say many of those people were still alive at the time he wrote 1 Corinthians two decades later.

Five hundred is not a large group. There are churches with choirs larger than that. For this purpose, however, the number is just right.

How many disciples did Jesus have during his ministry? The answer depends on what is meant by "disciple." The first answer that comes to mind is twelve; but there were many more, and they seemed to comprise a set of concentric rings of involvement. A list might look like this:

- The inner circle comprising Peter, James, and John
- The twelve including the inner circle and the nine other disciples
- The seventy: "After this, the Lord appointed 70 others, and He sent them ahead of Him in pairs to every town and place where He Himself was about to go" (Luke 10:1).
- The one hundred twenty: "During these days Peter stood up among the brothers—the number of people who were together was about 120" (Acts 1:15).
- The five hundred

Eleven of the original twelve disciples would become apostles, but so did a man named Matthias who was elected by the remaining eleven to replace Judas. He is interesting on two counts.

First, he was qualified to be an apostle because he had been with the group from the beginning. Peter listed the qualifications, saying, "Therefore, from among the men who have accompanied us during the whole time the Lord Jesus went in and out among us—beginning from the baptism of John until the day He was taken up from us—from among these, it is necessary that one become a witness with us of His resurrection" (Acts 1:21–22).

Another man was mentioned in Acts 1: "So they proposed two: Joseph, called Barsabbas, who was also known as Justus, and Matthias" (v. 23).

Justus and Matthias were there from Jesus' baptism to his ascension, yet this is the only place in the Bible where they are mentioned. Neither is ever heard from again—at least in the biblical record. Perhaps these men were numbered among the seventy.

A Closed Invitation

We've seen this verse before, but it has special meaning in this context. "God raised up this man on the third day and permitted Him to be seen, not by all the people, but by us, witnesses *appointed beforehand* by God, who ate and drank with Him after He rose from the dead" (Acts 10:40–41).

Chosen beforehand to be witnesses to the Resurrection. That certainly applies to the original disciples, the circle closest to Jesus. This was a special group. It did not include every believer, but those chosen to be eyewitnesses. This was a great honor, but it came with a price. Imagine telling your neighbors you have seen a man crucified and buried, now alive, walking and talking.

High-Level Meeting

This was a meeting of the highest level, literally and figuratively. The eleven disciples and others traveled north, back to the region of their home. Jesus had already appeared to them in Jerusalem, so why did he insist on the lengthy travel north? It was to include the five hundred. In Galilee, the followers of Christ could meet in greater safety than they could in Jerusalem.

Jesus' ministry was connected to mountains. He taught from them (Sermon on the Mount), prayed on them, retreated to them for rest, was transfigured on one, crucified on another, and commissioned his disciples and ascended to heaven from one (Mount of Olives).

On this unnamed mountain, Jesus appeared. The text in Matthew 28 states the disciples "saw Him," using a word that means to perceive with the senses, to see and understand (from *eido*). In other words, unlike Mary Magdalene's first encounter and the meeting on the road to Emmaus, they recognized Jesus immediately.

The sight of the risen Jesus walking their way drove them to their knees in worship. *Worship* (*proskyneō*) comes from a Greek word that means to "kiss toward." Picture the gathered disciples kneeling and blowing kisses toward the approaching Savior.

They knew this was an "official" meeting. Others had been casual and unexpected. This was a *called* meeting. They knew something was up.

They were right.

But before the meeting started, something had to be dealt with first.

Worship, Joy, and Persistent Doubt

"But some doubted" (Matt. 28:17). In the midst of worship stood those who had doubts. The word for doubt (*edistasan*) comes from two Greek words meaning "two" and "stand." In other words, Matthew, who was the only biblical writer to use the term, described doubt as standing in two ways. The image is of someone uncertain what to do or believe. The only other place this word is used in the Bible is Matthew 14:31, which records Peter's walk on water and near drowning. Jesus took the disciple by the hand, saving his life and asked, "You of little faith, why did you doubt?" In both cases the word is used when someone experiences Jesus in an unusual way.

Most likely the description is applied to some in the five hundred. The Eleven had already experienced the resurrected Jesus, but the others had not.

Doubt is a word that carries a lot of baggage. Often we hear doubt and equate it with disbelief. The idea here is not unbelief but conflict. Many were conflicted about what to believe. "Can it be true? Is that really Him?" *Dumbstruck* might be a better word.

I once did a radio interview for a Christian station during which "free thinkers" and skeptics are encouraged to call in.

One caller, an active pastor, asked me if I thought the Bible contained myth. I had to first determine what he meant by myth. (In some circles, myth refers to stories meant to teach a lesson. That definition would include biblical parables.) The caller made it clear that he was talking about fictional accounts—events that may not have happened but were included in the Bible to teach spiritual truths.

I responded by asserting my belief that the Bible is historically accurate and that all the events described in it occurred and were not fabrications. I did allow that parables were earthly stories with heavenly meanings and were useful teaching devices.

What struck me about his question was his honest admission that he was conflicted in his belief, yet every Sunday he had to stand in the pulpit and deliver a message based on a biblical text—a text he harbored doubts about.

Such doubts are not unusual. The Bible contains many mind-stretching accounts, events that are well beyond our normal experience. That does not make them any less true. Still, most of us have wrestled with doubts about spiritual issues, and in the long run that may be a very good thing. The more we wrestle with an issue the better we understand it.

Like that caller, some of the five hundred had issues about what they were seeing.

The One and Only

Whatever doubts and inner conflicts existed, they were put to rest by the approach of Jesus. "Then Jesus came near" (v. 18a). What a wonderful truth: Christ is proactive.

Leadership literature teaches there are three types of action: inaction, reaction, and proaction. Jesus was never inactive or reactive. Everything he did, he did with purpose. That includes his passive acceptance of illegal trials and physical brutality. During those horrible hours, he was not inactive, he was enduring the very thing he had come to endure.

The text tells us "Jesus came near." The visual is of Jesus crossing the distance that separated him from the crowd of disciples and walking into their midst. He did not stand at a distance to proclaim his message; he waded into their midst. It was a very physical thing to do. Everyone could see with his own eyes that Christ was raised bodily, that he was just as physical in the Resurrection as he was before his death.

Then Jesus spoke: "All authority has been given to Me in heaven and on earth. Go, therefore, and make disciples of all nations, baptizing them in the name of the Father and of the Son and of the Holy Spirit, teaching them to observe everything I have commanded you. And remember, I am with you always, to the end of the age" (vv. 18b–20).

First, he spoke about himself: "All authority has been given to Me." *Authority* appears more than one hundred times in the New Testament and refers to the power of choice. It's the kind of statement a leader would make as he assumes control. Jesus was stating that he is in charge and not just of those around him, but of all heaven and earth. Jesus rules over a kingdom without borders. He rules over heaven, a kingdom invisible to us, and earth, the place we live.

Then Jesus spoke about them. In a sense, the baton was being passed, not just to the eleven disciples, but to the hundreds who gathered around to hear his words. This was an executive meeting wherein Christ laid out the task for these believers—and the task was enormous. A. T. Robertson had his finger on the pulse of Jesus' command when he wrote, "Risen Christ without money or army or state charging this band of five hundred men and women with world conquest and bringing them to believe it possible and to undertake it with serious passion and power. Pentecost is still to come, but dynamic faith rules on this mountain in Galilee."[2]

From the Mountain to the World

These verses, often called the Great Commission, are well known to churchgoers. For many, it is the command to evangelize the world, and they are not far wrong. Often overlooked, however, is Jesus' primary command.

I stood before a group of pastors in Southern California. I was there to teach a seminar on change dynamics in the church. Before me were men who had spent many years in training and possessed decades of experience. I asked, "What is the primary goal of the church?" The answer came quickly: "To evangelize, to win the lost."

They were surprised when I told them they were wrong—not very wrong—but a little off course. "But that's what the Great Commission says," one of the brothers protested.

"Is it? Let's look." I reminded them that Jesus' command was not to evangelize the lost but to make disciples. It seems a small distinction, but it is much more. Winning the lost is not the goal; it is the first step in a process. The goal has always been to make disciples, followers, committed learners, people whose lives are different because of their faith.

All too often, people are led to Christ and left to float on the waves of ignorance. Jesus commanded his followers to replicate themselves in the lives of others, that is, to guide others into discipleship who would in turn disciple others. The first step is evangelism, but leading someone to Christ was never meant to be the end, rather the beginning.

The command to *go* must have been shocking. They were to make "disciples of all nations." In a world without electronics, in a time when the fastest a person could travel was by chariot, the command to move into other nations was stunning.

This work was to include baptizing and "teaching them to observe everything I have commanded you." That is the definition of disciple making—teaching people how to observe (keep) the commands of Christ.

Then Jesus made a promise: "And remember, I am with you always, to the end of the age" (v. 20). Those last words must have been comforting to a people asked to leave home and hearth for the world.

The Commission Turned Inward

At an evangelism conference in central California, I sat among hundreds of pastors as I listened to Andy Anderson—Mr. Sunday School—deliver a heart-stirring message. During that sermon he quoted the Twenty-third Psalm in a way I had never heard before. He reversed everything and called it the lost-person's psalm. I have never forgotten it.

> The LORD is *not* my shepherd; I shall *forever* want.
>
> He *doesn't* maketh me to lie down in green pastures: he *doesn't* lead me beside the still waters.

> He *doesn't* restore my soul: he leadeth me *not* in the paths of righteousness for his name's sake.
>
> Yea, though I walk through the valley of the shadow of death, I will fear *every* evil: for thou art *not* with me; thy rod and thy staff they *do not* comfort me.
>
> Thou preparest *not* a table before me in the presence of mine enemies: thou anointest *not* my head with oil; my cup *never* runneth over.
>
> Surely goodness and mercy shall *avoid* me all the days of my life: and I will *never* dwell in the house of the LORD (adapted from the KJV; italics indicate insertions).

Such Bible gymnastics can be useful in helping us see something new in familiar passages. When we come to the Great Commission passage, we see new light by turning it inward. Certainly Jesus meant for us to understand the need for going out to make disciples, but that journey must first be made inward. To make a disciple, we must be a disciple, committed learner, and doer. Before we can encourage others to follow Christ in baptism, we must first pass through those waters ourselves. To teach, we must first learn. To proclaim Jesus, we must first know him.

The talented musician and performer Steve Green penned a wonderful song in which he encourages Christians to live and work in such a way that those who come after will find us faithful. That is the lesson of the Great Commission.

Sometimes the first person we win to Christ is ourselves. Only then can we go.

Chapter 13

Breakfast by the Sea

From time to time, children must go to the doctor or the dentist. It can be frightening, especially sitting in the lobby, waiting to be called to those mysterious rooms in the back. Today, children find a magazine in most waiting rooms that helps them keep their minds off what lies ahead. It's the same magazine that many of us read when we were children. *Highlights for Children* has been around for many years. I recall biding my time, playing one of the games in the magazine's pages. It was a find-the-picture game. A page was filled with a scene, the big picture, but "buried" in the lines of the drawings were outlines of objects. The magazine challenged me to find the hammer, the bird, the car, the barbecue, and more. Some were easy to find; others took more work. I learned that if I looked hard, I could find every hidden object.

Portions of the Bible are that way. There is a pattern to Scripture and symbolism "hidden" just below the surface. With a little practice, we see not only the overall picture but also the smaller ones nestled inside. Below is one of those passages I suspect has more meaning than we realize. If we look closer and delve deeper, we see not only the surface lesson but a very creative statement about Jesus and his ministry.

Let's take a look at the provocative set of circumstances surrounding the eighth close encounter with Christ.

> After this, Jesus revealed Himself again to His disciples by the Sea of Tiberias. He revealed Himself in this way:
>
> Simon Peter, Thomas (called "Twin"), Nathanael from Cana of Galilee, Zebedee's sons, and two others of His disciples were together.
>
> "I'm going fishing," Simon Peter said to them.
>
> "We're coming with you," they told him. They went out and got into the boat, but that night they caught nothing.
>
> When daybreak came, Jesus stood on the shore. However, the disciples did not know it was Jesus.
>
> "Men," Jesus called to them, "you don't have any fish, do you?"
>
> "No," they answered.
>
> "Cast the net on the right side of the boat," He told them, "and you'll find some." So they did, and they were unable to haul it in because of the large number of fish. Therefore the disciple, the one Jesus loved, said to Peter, "It is the Lord!"
>
> When Simon Peter heard that it was the Lord, he tied his outer garment around him (for he was

stripped) and plunged into the sea. But since they were not far from land (about 100 yards away), the other disciples came in the boat, dragging the net full of fish. When they got out on land, they saw a charcoal fire there, with fish lying on it, and bread.

"Bring some of the fish you've just caught," Jesus told them. So Simon Peter got up and hauled the net ashore, full of large fish—153 of them. Even though there were so many, the net was not torn.

"Come and have breakfast," Jesus told them. None of the disciples dared ask Him, "Who are You?" because they knew it was the Lord. Jesus came, took the bread, and gave it to them. He did the same with the fish.

This was now the third time Jesus appeared to the disciples after He was raised from the dead. (John 21:1–14)

An "Acted Parable"

The first three Gospels contain the parables of Jesus. There are about thirty such stories to illustrate and make memorable a spiritual truth. A parable is a story laid alongside a truth to make the truth easier to understand. In a sense, a parable is an everyday story with a forever lesson attached. Jesus used parables to separate those who wanted to know from those who didn't. Understanding a parable takes brain work.

The parables in the Gospels were told by the Teacher to those who came to hear him. But there is another type of parable, what I call an "acted parable." These were events Jesus created to drive home a point. Baptism and the Lord's Supper are two examples. These lessons were taught without lectures—sermons preached without words.

On the shores of the Sea of Galilee, Jesus taught a magnificent lesson with a miracle and breakfast.

The early encounters with Christ happened in and around Jerusalem. Then he appeared to the Eleven and the five hundred on a mountain in Galilee. Away from Jerusalem, the disciples felt freer to move in public. Peter decided to go fishing, and why not? This was his old stomping grounds, and now he was, for the moment, free to do so. Fishing would be an emotional release, and some of the other disciples decided to go with him. They included Peter's partners from his fishing business, James and John, the sons of Zebedee; Nathanael (Bartholomew); Thomas; and two unnamed disciples. It's possible that one of the unnamed disciples was Andrew, Peter's brother, and the other Philip, the friend of Nathanael.

This was meaningful territory for the disciples. Of Jesus' thirty-plus parables, nineteen were told in Galilee; of his thirty-three miracles, twenty-five were performed there. This was home to the disciples and served as headquarters for Christ's early ministry.

It must have felt good to be back on the water again, especially after three challenging years of ministry and the horrible stress of the past few weeks.

As usual, the fishing was done at night. Hour after hour, they cast their nets and came up empty. Fishermen of the day used three types of nets. One was the dragnet usually worked by teams in two boats. The large net would be stretched between the craft then drawn together, trapping the fish inside. Another kind of net was the bag net, used for deep fishing. The net would be lowered into the depths where it would open. The fishermen would then draw the net to the surface. The net would "bag" the fish. The type of nets used in this situation were most likely cast nets (*diktuon*), tossed from the side of the boat and reeled in by hand. When Jesus first called Peter, James, and John to be disciples, they had just finished cleaning and repairing these kinds of nets (Luke 5:2).

As Jesus had drawn these men into the ministry three years before, he again approached them by the seashore. He made an uncommon appearance in a common situation.

He called out to them, asking a question; he already knew the answer: "Men, you don't have any fish, do you?" (John 21:5). Here things got interesting. First, Jesus didn't use the word for "men"; instead, he called them *paidia,* children. The word was used to describe an infant or small child (we get our English word *pediatric* from it).

Jesus asked if they had any "fish." Strictly speaking, Jesus didn't use the word for fish in his question (he did later). He asked, "Boys, have you anything to add?" Jesus used a Greek word that's difficult to translate: *prosphagion.* It refers to anything eaten with bread, from relish to fried fish.

Once again, Peter and the others had to admit failure at something that was once their livelihood. No fisherman likes to admit "getting skunked."

Jesus gave familiar advice: "Cast the net on the right side of the boat, . . . and you'll find some" (v. 6). Fish off the other side. It was a nonsensical suggestion.

When I was a teenager, I would go to the Ocean Beach pier in San Diego and fish. It was an enjoyable time with my friends. It was also a place I gained insight into the odd psychology of some people. It was amazing to watch people. If someone caught a good-sized fish on the north side of the pier, people on the south side would move their gear to join him—on a pier that wasn't more than twenty-five feet across. Professionals like Peter would see the recommendation as foolish, but they had been surprised before.

They were surprised again.

Details, Details

The nets hit the water and sank with their weights. The disciples pulled the drawstring, and to their astonishment the nets were heavy with fish. John, described here as "the one Jesus loved," made the connection: "It is the Lord!"

With that, Peter, too, put it all together and no longer cared about fishing. He leaped from the boat and began swimming to shore, leaving the great haul of fish to the others. Peter had left fish behind before to follow Jesus.

The disciples finished drawing in the catch, then rowed to shore. Peter, perhaps feeling guilty for leaving his friends to do the hard work, pulled the net on shore. Here the details become fascinating. Unfortunately, most are missed in the English translations.

First, when the disciples were on land again, they noticed a charcoal fire and a fish cooking on it. The word for fish is singular. It's just one fish. Not only that, the word used (*opsarion*) most likely means a small fish. So Peter and the others saw a bed of coals, a single small fish lying on it as well as bread.

This brings us to a question: Why did John record Jesus using a different word for fish than expected? The only other place John used that term is in his account of the feeding of the five thousand (6:9–11). If we were reading the Gospel of John in the original language, we would first come across the feeding of the multitudes with five loaves and two fish (*opsarion*), then reach this account and see that John used the same word. Our thoughts would snap back to that event and realize that Jesus was multiplying the fish and bread for the disciples and making a statement at the same time.

Oddly, Jesus told them to bring some of the fish (*opsarioon*) they caught. Peter went, dragged the net ashore, and counted out 153 large fish (*ichthuoon*). (We get our word *ichthyology,* the study of fish, from the root of this word.) This use of alternating terms continues through the passage. Charted it looks like this:

Association/POV	Term	Number
Jesus (v. 5)	prosphagion	singular
Disciples (v. 6)	ichthuoon	plural
Disciples (v. 8)	ichthuoon	plural
Jesus (v. 9)	opsarion	singular
Jesus speaking (v. 10)	opsarioon	plural
Peter (v. 11)	ichthuoon	plural
Jesus (v. 13)	opsarion	singular

In this passage, Jesus repeatedly used *opsarion* to refer to fish while the author John used *ichthuoon.* Also, this fish associated with Jesus is always singular, that associated with the disciple is always plural.

This may seem like we're torturing the text, but such details are no accident. The question is why John, under the inspiration of the Holy Spirit, made such subtle distinctions and included such details about the number of fish caught.

This last question has been asked for centuries, and some odd ideas have been put forth. Some have seen the number of fish matching the number of nations; Cyril of Alexandria suggested that the one hundred represented the Gentiles, the fifty referred to the Jews, and the three was a reference to the Trinity. Then there was Augustine, Bishop of Hippo, who concluded that if one adds 1+2+3 . . . 17, he would arrive at 153, and that if the fish were laid out with one fish in the first row, two in the second, and so on, a perfect triangle would be formed and the triangle would represent the Trinity.

Perhaps there is some special meaning in 153, but most likely John included the number as historical fact and to contrast with the one fish Jesus had. It was customary to divide up a catch. Peter's counting of the fish would be second nature, something he did while separating one kind of fish from another.

The risen Jesus then invited the men to breakfast. While he sent them to bring some of the fish they had caught, there was no mention of those being prepared to eat. Instead, "Jesus came, took the bread, and gave it to them. He did the same with the fish" (v. 13).

A small fish and a single loaf of bread divided among seven disciples. There was a miracle here. The Gospels record five miracles by Jesus that involved fish. Three of them were feedings. In one case he fed five thousand Jews; in another he multiplied fish and bread for three thousand Gentiles, and here he did the same for seven hungry disciples.

Seeing this act would drive the minds of the disciples back to those events, which they not only witnessed but helped perform. Jesus provided for the needs of the crowds with a tiny amount of food, and now he provided for the needs of the disciples. Jesus promised they would become fishers of men, and they were about to become just that.

The Parable's Lesson

This is an acted parable. Jesus did more than recite a story; he created an unforgettable setting that would remind the disciples of the past.

Things had changed. In the days ahead, Jesus would ascend to heaven and would not be showing up on the seashore, in the Upper Room, or on a road that led to Emmaus or any other town. They would have to move ahead, knowing Christ was with them whether they saw him or not.

They also needed to know that although it would seem as if they failed, Jesus would bring success. They would still have to be in the boat, still throw the nets, and still pull beyond their strength, but they would not do this alone. Jesus would be watching and helping. The breakfast would remind them God would always provide.

I pull another lesson from this. Jesus is working even when we don't recognize him doing so. From their spot in the boat, the disciples did not recognize Jesus, but they followed through on his advice. Only after the great catch did they make the connection.

It is impossible to know how many times Jesus has done something to our benefit and we haven't recognized it, but that doesn't mean he's been inactive. The key is knowing we are not in this life alone. We may not see Jesus in the flesh, but that does nothing to diminish his power.

When we're in the boat, he's on the shore watching and giving advice; and one day we'll find ourselves on the same shore, and it will be Jesus who serves us what we need.

Chapter 14

A Family Visit

Some of the most complicated relationships are family ones. While the United Nations struggles to keep nations acting responsibly and friendly toward one another, a similar battle goes on in the homes of the world. Statistics tells us that about half of all American marriages will end in divorce. Sibling rivalry changes family bonds into competition. Nothing new here. The Bible is filled with families damaged by greed, mistrust, or just plain stupidity.

Often we assume that Jesus' family was free of such pettiness, but it wasn't. Not only, as Jesus told us, is a prophet without honor in his hometown, but apparently he received no more respect at home than he did elsewhere.

We have seen one of the shortest recorded appearances of Christ when we examined Jesus' first appearance to Peter. All we have is, "'The Lord has certainly been raised, and has appeared to Simon!'" (Luke 24:34). The Bible records another secret meeting among the appearances of Christ, this one to a family member, a brother named James. "Then He appeared to James" (1 Cor. 15:7a). That's it, the whole account in five words in the English translation and just three words in the original Greek.

Leslie Lemke is an unusual musician. At age fourteen, he played Tchaikovsky's *Piano Concerto no. 1* with flawless panache. It was a piece of music he had heard only once before. Remarkable as that is, it is a small thing when compared to the fact that he is blind, developmentally disabled, and has cerebral palsy. He sings and plays in concerts in the United States and around the world. Lemke has never had a piano lesson.

Richard Wawro is an internationally known artist. Margaret Thatcher and Pope John Paul II collected his work. One art professor said he was "thunderstruck" by the young man's work. Richard Wawro is autistic and unable to communicate with anyone.

Kim Peek was made famous by Dustin Hoffman's portrayal of him in the movie *Rain Man.* Peek has memorized 7,600 books, can recite the name of every city in the United States and all the highways that connect them as well as their area codes, zip codes, and television and radio stations. Tell him your birthday, and he will tell you what day of the week you were born and the day of the week you will turn sixty-five. He can recognize most classical music and give the composer's name and birth and death dates as well as when the music was first published or performed. He is developmentally disabled and depends on his father for his daily needs. He cannot live on his own.

Amazing, isn't it, that these men and others like them can be so dysfunctional in most areas of life but excel in others? Their condition is called savant syndrome.

Benjamin Rush did research with such people as early as 1789. He met one young man who was asked how many seconds a man would live if he lived seventy years, seventeen days, and twelve hours. Ninety seconds later, came the answer: 2,210,500,800 seconds . . . and he took into account seventeen leap years.

These people are remarkable for the odd pairing of great ability with great disability. They excel in a few things but miss the whole world.

Who Was James?

James, the half brother of Jesus, was an ordinary man who saw the whole world but missed the exceptional . . . then became exceptional himself. His is a story of change, of migration from disbelief to faith.

Barely Mentioned in the Gospels

He may have lived in the same home as Jesus, watching his older brother grow, but he is all but absent from the Gospels, being mentioned only twice.

"Isn't this the carpenter's son? Isn't His mother called Mary, and His brothers James, Joseph, Simon, and Judas?" (Matt. 13:55; also see Mark 6:3).

This comment was made in response to some of Jesus' miracles. Many were trying to reconcile the miracles they had seen with a man whose family they knew.

Since James is mentioned first in both accounts, he may have been the oldest of Jesus' siblings, the oldest brother. If this was true, he would have been the family leader. Most scholars assume that Joseph, Mary's husband, died sometime after Jesus turned twelve. The last time we see him is in Luke 2:41–50 when young Jesus was left behind at the temple. Joseph is never mentioned again. If he did indeed die between that event and the start of Jesus' ministry, Jesus, as the oldest, would have become the head of the household. After Jesus left home to begin his three-year ministry, that task would fall next to James.

He was never numbered among the disciples and, as we will see, was a skeptic.

Apparently Married

As a typical Jewish man, marriage was in his future. The apostle Paul posed a question that indicates James was married: "Don't we have the right to be accompanied by a Christian wife, like the other apostles, the Lord's brothers, and Cephas?" (1 Cor. 9:5).

James was a family man. The best we can tell, he was an "everyman" living an everyday life. He had responsibilities, duties, and obligations typical of a first-century Jewish man. In many ways, he was like the rest of us.

Except he had a brother named Jesus.

Was a Skeptic

Seems like an odd statement, doesn't it? How could someone who grew up so close to Jesus not recognize his unique nature? We have no answer to that question.

Two verses drive this fact home: "When His family heard this, they set out to restrain Him, because they said, 'He's out of His mind'" (Mark 3:21) and "For not even His brothers believed in Him" (John 7:5).

"He is out of His mind." What a piercing sentence. We can only guess how much such a statement hurt Jesus. Leading that attempt to take "protective custody" of Jesus was James. He was the head of the household. The word for "restrain" (from *krateo*) means to take by force. They were going to physically "arrest" Jesus. Not even Jesus could count on family. His words and we assume those of Mary were unable to convince his siblings of his real nature. Those closest to him were the furthest away.

James was a skeptic when it came to Jesus. For some reason, he could not see what needed to be seen. Perhaps he was a skeptic by nature. I read of an accounting firm that had the slogan "In God We Trust. All Others We Audit." James would have fit in well there.

Skepticism can be blinding. Imagine what James almost missed. The good news is he didn't miss it.

Became a Believer

Somewhere along the line, James and his siblings had a change of heart. The Bible doesn't tell us where or when, but after the death and resurrection of Jesus, we find him with the disciples and others in prayer. "All these were continually united in prayer, along with the women, including Mary the mother of Jesus, and His brothers" (Acts 1:14).

We know of James's conversion but not the details. He had a close encounter with Christ and was forever changed.

The details are kept private and so is the information about Jesus' appearance to James. Only Paul mentioned it in those few words, "Then He appeared to James." So few words for such an important man. We assume this was the point of persuasion, the event that turned James around.

The important proof is not in the event but in the change that followed. He went from disbelief to belief, no small step for a man who previously considered Jesus mentally unbalanced.

Skeptics sometimes make the best believers. History is filled with those who doubted the claims of Christ only to become his champion. Saul of Tarsus, who persecuted the church, became the apostle Paul, the greatest missionary in history; Augustine was an immoral youth who became one of the church's great thinkers and bishop of Hippo; Charles Colson was changed from Watergate conspirator to founder of Prison Fellowship Ministries; C. S. Lewis went from atheism to defending the faith in books and on radio. James would morph from skeptical brother to the head of the Jerusalem church.

Considered an Apostle

James's meeting with the risen Christ changed the future. Where once he stood among the doubters, James rose to a place of prominence in church history. In describing his Christian journey, the apostle Paul said, "But I didn't see any of the other apostles except James, the Lord's brother" (Gal. 1:19).

Paul referred to James as an apostle. Apostle is a special designation for a close follower of Christ, one who held a special position in the first-century church. There is some irony here. As we saw earlier, the disciples elected Matthias to replace Judas. Scholars agree it was a hasty move. They were running ahead of God. Still, we see the requirements for an apostle in Peter's speech: "Therefore, from among the men who have accompanied us during the whole time the Lord Jesus went in and out among us—beginning from the baptism of John until the day He was taken up from us—from among these, it is necessary that one become a witness with us of His resurrection" (Acts 1:21–22).

It is doubtful that James would have met these stipulations, yet Paul and others considered him an apostle. (For that matter, Paul failed to meet Peter's criteria.) A man named Barnabas, the early partner in ministry with Paul, was referred to as an apostle (Acts 14:14). The point is: men don't select apostles, Jesus does.

Tradition holds that Jesus personally commissioned James as an apostle and set him among the leaders of the church. Something happened for others to see James as a believer and leader rather than the skeptical brother.

Leader of the Church in Jerusalem

There's no way to tell how rapid a rise James had. We know that Paul appeared before him at the Jerusalem church, and most scholars date Paul's conversion close to the beginning of the church. From there he spent time away from Jerusalem. By the time he arrived in Jerusalem to meet with the church's leadership, James had replaced Peter as "senior pastor."

Paul spoke of James again in Galatians 2:9: "When James, Cephas, and John, recognized as pillars, acknowledged the grace that had been given to me, they gave the right hand of fellowship to me and Barnabas, [agreeing] that we should go to the Gentiles and they to the circumcised."

James's rise to the top was quick, happening in only a few years. Early church historian Eusebius said that James was appointed first bishop of Jerusalem by the Lord himself.[1]

James would also author the Epistle of James, one of the most direct books of the New Testament. In that book, he described himself as "James, a slave of God and of the Lord Jesus Christ" (1:1).

Clearly his personal and private meeting with the resurrected Christ left him a changed man.

Died for His Faith

Faith comes with a price, and for James the cost would be paid with his life. After decades of service to Christ, he was martyred. The Jewish historian Josephus and the Christian Hegesippus (according to the fourth-century church historian Eusebius) reported that James was put to death by the priestly authorities in Jerusalem a few years before the destruction of the temple in AD 70.

Josephus put it this way: "Festus was now dead, and Albinus was but upon the road; so he assembled the Sanhedrin of judges, and brought before them the brother of Jesus, who was called Christ, whose name was James, and some others, [or, some of his companions]; and when he had formed an accusation against them as breakers of the law, he delivered them to be stoned."[2]

It was a long way from wanting to restrain Jesus to dying for him by stoning.

We have no idea where the resurrected Jesus met James. No clues are given about the words spoken or how long the meeting lasted. We do know that a critic became a believer and in turn became a pillar of the church and one of its greatest martyrs. In James's case, he had a close encounter with Jesus of the family kind.

Lessons

The most touching aspect of this encounter is Jesus' willingness to approach a family member in private and make yet another effort to convince him of the truth. Just as he recovered Peter after his denial, Jesus took James aside, and the man and the world were forever changed.

The only history we have of Jesus' other half siblings is the author of the tiny New Testament book of Jude. The book begins, "Jude, a slave of Jesus Christ, and a brother of James" (Jude 1). James became a follower and so did Jude, also known as Judas (not Iscariot the traitor).

If James could move from doubter to believer, anyone can. During Christ's ministry, James may have wondered how to distance himself and his family from Jesus; then after the Resurrection, he wondered how best to serve him.

Jesus moved him out of the shadows and into the light of leadership. It's amazing how often God chooses the least likely people to be the most successful in his work.

The move from hindrance to important player impacted the lives of countless people. James may have been stoned to death for his faith in the first century, but his contribution, especially the Bible book that bears his name, continues to change lives in the twenty-first century.

The Indian reformer and pacifist Mahatma Gandhi is reputed to have said, "I'd become a Christian if it weren't for the Christians." Like James, we all need to move from being hindrances to important players. Important means doing whatever it is that God has called you to do.

Perhaps there is another lesson here. Many of us have faced the sad problem of having unbelievers in our families. It's a painful realization. In prayer meetings around the world, people request prayer for the salvation of a brother, husband, sister, aunt, or wife. The anxiety is clear in their voices. During my ministry, I have heard countless people express the same sentiment: "You'll never see my husband [father, wife, brother, etc.] in church." Over the years, I have been blessed to watch those "impossibilities" not only come to church, but come to Christ and begin years of service.

There was a time when James might have said, "You'll never see me following Jesus," but he did. He changed because Jesus rose from the dead. Jesus hadn't given up on his half brother, and he hasn't given up on anyone you know.

Chapter 15

The Big Exit

Thomas Jefferson was a man of rare talent, keen intellect, and strong leadership. Architect, farmer, statesman, president, he most wanted to be known as an educator. Nothing was beyond his scrutiny—not even the Bible. So, with quill in hand, the great man began to "improve" the New Testament.

He started with the belief that the Gospels had been contaminated by ancient Greek philosophy. His solution? Cut out the stuff that didn't belong. Eighteen hundred years after the New Testament had been penned, Jefferson felt he was the better judge for what was true and what was corruption.

He described this work as "abstracting what is really his [Jesus'] from the rubbish in which it is buried, easily distinguished by its luster from the dross of his biographers, and as separate from that as the diamond from the dung hill."[1]

When he was done, all references to the supernatural had been cut away—no mention of the virgin birth, the appearance of angels, and the Resurrection. Jefferson had confined himself solely to the moral teachings of Jesus and tossed aside the miracles and references to the supernatural.

The closing words of Jefferson's Bible are: "There laid they Jesus and rolled a great stone at the mouth of the sepulcher and departed."

The Resurrection has been a problem for many people. It stretches their minds too far and asks them to step into the light of reasoned faith. That changes nothing. The Resurrection is a fact of history that continues to change lives.

The Bible is as God intended it to be and includes dramatic, supernatural events. Perhaps no such event is more dramatic than Jesus' "liftoff" from earth to heaven. "Then He led them out as far as Bethany, and lifting up His hands He blessed them. And while He was blessing them, He left them *and was carried up into heaven.* After worshiping Him, they returned to Jerusalem with great joy. And they were continually in the temple complex blessing God" (Luke 24:50–53).

What a sight that must have been. This event is recorded in two of the four Gospels (see Mark 16:19) and in the book of Acts (1:4–11). It is also mentioned in other New Testament books:

> Now that He has *gone into heaven,* He is at God's right hand, with angels, authorities, and powers subjected to Him. (1 Pet. 3:22)
>
> And most certainly, the mystery of godliness is great:
>
> He was manifested in the flesh,
> justified in the Spirit,
> seen by angels,

> preached among the Gentiles,
> believed on in the world,
> *taken up in glory.* (1 Tim. 3:16)
>
> Therefore since we have a great high priest who has *passed through the heavens*—Jesus the Son of God—let us hold fast to the confession. (Heb. 4:14)

The ascension of Christ was unique because it was not only a resurrection appearance but a disappearance.

The Place He Chose

Bethany was a town familiar to Jesus and the disciples. He spent a great deal of time there; his friends Lazarus, Mary, and Martha were residents. Jesus often stayed there when his ministry took him to Jerusalem.

Why did Jesus take his disciples to Bethany? There are practical reasons. First, it was just two miles outside of Jerusalem and on one of the slopes of the Mount of Olives. The disciples returned to Jerusalem as ordered by Jesus and after the Ascension were to remain there until they received power from the Holy Spirit, an event described in Acts 2.

Bethany had served as the local headquarters for Jesus during the final days of his ministry. The Triumphal Entry into Jerusalem began in Bethany, an act that portrayed Christ as Messiah. At Bethany a woman anointed Jesus with oil. When some complained about the extravagant waste (the anointing oil was very expensive), Jesus chastised the complainers and added, "She has done what she could; she has anointed My body in advance for burial" (Mark 14:8).

By raising Lazarus from the dead, Jesus demonstrated the power he had over death and foreshadowed his own permanent rise from the dead.

Bethany was also the last stop on the pilgrim's path to Jerusalem and a fitting, symbolic locale to show the end of Jesus' earthly ministry.

Places have meaning in the story of Christ, and Bethany was a key place.

The Blessing He Gave

"Lifting up His hands He blessed them" (Luke 24:50b).

I've wondered what went through the minds of the disciples as they walked that last two miles with Jesus. The passage reveals, "He led them out as far as Bethany," indicating that Jesus appeared to them in Jerusalem and walked the two miles with them.

Did they chat? Were they full of questions? Did anxiety and fear rage within them, or was the presence of Jesus enough to calm their uncertainty? Surely they knew something was up, something of great significance. Jesus had appeared to them in closed rooms, on a mountainside, by the seashore, in private with Peter, then with his brother James, by the tomb, and the roadway. Now he led them from the Holy City to the slopes of the Mount of Olives. It was on the mount that Jesus' greatest agony occurred in the Garden of Gethsemane. Now his greatest glory would occur here.

Once at the chosen spot, Jesus raised his hands and blessed them. This is the only time in the Gospels Jesus is said to have lifted his hands. There is poignant irony here.

Two miles away, just outside of Jerusalem, Jesus' enemies raised his hands and nailed them to the cross. He allowed them to do so. Now he raised nail-scarred hands to bless those who fled in the face of the horrible danger. The eyes of everyone would be fixed on those wounds.

His final words were of blessing. How interesting. "And while He was blessing them, He left them and was carried up into heaven" (Luke 24:51). As he spoke the words, Jesus rose into the air.

I used to picture Jesus rising to heaven with his face turned toward the sky, his eyes set on the destination, but this passage has corrected me. Instead of seeing Jesus rise into the air with his back turned on the disciples like a man leaving friends behind as he walks down a road, we see Jesus facing his friends as he is lifted from the earth. His attention was on them—attentive in the last moments.

Neither the Gospels nor the book of Acts tell what Jesus said, but we have an idea. God himself wrote the words used to bless the Israelites. Those words were given to Moses to pass on to Aaron:

> Tell Aaron and his sons how you are to bless the Israelites. Say to them:
>
> "The LORD bless you and protect you;
> the LORD make His face shine on you,
> and be gracious to you;
> the LORD look with favor on you
> and give you peace."
>
> In this way they will put My name on the Israelites, and I will bless them. (Num. 6:23–27)

This was much more than a polite act. Jesus was doing the work of the High Priest. Originally, it was the first high priest Aaron who pronounced the blessing on the people of Israel; and now Jesus, the forever High Priest, did the same. We don't know the exact words, but it is reasonable to suppose that Jesus spoke the same words used by Aaron centuries before.

This is even more intriguing when we realize Aaron not only blessed the people, but he did so at a special time. "Aaron lifted up his hands toward the people and blessed them. He came down after sacrificing the sin offering, the burnt offering, and the fellowship offering" (Lev. 9:22).

Aaron blessed the people *after* he had made the sacrifices for them, including the sin offering. Jesus was that offering on the cross. What may seem an interesting bit of Bible trivia to us, the Jewish disciples would have immediately understood and perhaps had been stunned. Jesus was doing work only the high priest was allowed to do and very likely using the same words God had given Aaron.

That wasn't Jesus' final blessing. Paul wrote to the church in Ephesus, "Blessed be the God and Father of our Lord Jesus Christ, who has blessed us with every spiritual blessing in the heavens, in Christ; for He chose us in Him, before the foundation of the world, to be holy and blameless in His sight" (Eph. 1:3–4).

So what were the disciples to do in such a situation? Those disciples worshiped him and "returned to Jerusalem with great joy" (Luke 24:52). We might expect sadness. After all, Jesus had left them. Instead, we see an outpouring of praise and joy. They were starting to get it.

The two shortest verses in the Bible are 1 Thessalonians 5:16, "Rejoice always!" and John 11:35, "Jesus wept." Odd, isn't it? One deals with sorrow, the other with joy. When it came to these powerhouse emotions, few words were needed to express what was felt.

They understood what they witnessed, and the natural thing to do was worship, express joy, and let loose with public praise. The more we know about Jesus and his resurrection, the more we will do those three things. The closer we nestle to the truth, the greater the joy.

The Way He Left

Jesus' departure seems surprising, but it shouldn't be. Jesus spoke of his ascension almost as much as he spoke of his death. The Gospel of John records several times when Jesus spoke in advance of his departure.

> Jesus, knowing in Himself that His disciples were complaining about this, asked them, "Does this offend you? *Then what if you were to observe the Son of Man ascending to where He was before?"* (6:61–62)
>
> Then Jesus said, "I am only with you for a short time. *Then I'm going to the One who sent Me.* You will look for Me, but you will not find Me; and where I am, you cannot come." (7:33–34)
>
> "You have heard Me tell you, 'I am going away and I am coming to you.' If you loved Me, you would have rejoiced that I am going to the Father,

> because the Father is greater than I. I have told you now before it happens so that when it does happen you may believe. I will not talk with you much longer, because the ruler of the world is coming. He has no power over Me. On the contrary, *I am going away so that the world may know that I love the Father.* Just as the Father commanded Me, so I do." (14:28–31a)

In the first recorded appearance of Christ after his death, a grieving Mary Magdalene seized Jesus' feet, clinging for all she was worth. "Don't cling to Me," Jesus told her, "for I have not yet ascended to the Father" (John 20:17).

Before the Crucifixion, Jesus made no secret of the events to transpire. He would be betrayed by one of his disciples, handed over to his enemies, suffer greatly, be crucified, then rise from the dead, and later ascend to the Father.

Before their eyes, while Jesus was blessing them, the disciples and others saw Jesus rise from the ground and continue to ascend until they could no longer see him. The Resurrection was physical in every respect and so was the Ascension.

The Bible records the event by saying that Jesus "was carried up into heaven." All mentions of this are in the passive. In other words, it was done to Jesus, not by Jesus. The Father raised him to heaven where he disappeared in a cloud.

One More Thing

Luke recorded the event in his book of Acts, the companion book to the Gospel of Luke. He added exciting details:

"After He had said this, He was taken up as they were watching, and a cloud received Him out of their sight. While He was going, they were gazing into heaven, and suddenly two men in white clothes stood by them. They said, 'Men of Galilee, why do you stand looking up into heaven? This Jesus, who has been taken from you into heaven, will come in the same way that you have seen Him going into heaven'" (1:9–11).

There's an old saying, "What goes up must come down." Here in this stunning moment when Jesus rose from the sight of the disciples, two angels delivered a reminder. Just as an angel announced to Mary that she would bear the child Jesus, just as angels announced his birth, just as angels announced Christ's resurrection, so now they stated facts known to them: Jesus will return in a similar fashion as the disciples saw him go.

Look at the facts they reveal. First, Jesus' return would be as real as his ascension. There was no doubt or hedging in their words. Most likely these words were delivered to the eleven disciples because the angels referred to them as "men of Galilee," and all the remaining disciples were Galileans. They were far from home, in hostile territory. The angels' first words reminded them of their origins.

Next, they stated the fact of Jesus' return as easily as if they were calling the sky blue. Jesus will return. No doubts. No conditions. But no timetable either. That knowledge remains proprietary with God.

Jesus' return would be in the same fashion as his departure: "This Jesus, who has been taken from you into heaven, will come in the same way that you have seen Him going into heaven" (v. 11b). Jesus will return from the sky to the earth, from a place shielded from the eyes of humans to our full vision.

Since Jesus' resurrection and ascension were bodily, so will his return be. Not only will the manner of his return be the same, but he will touch down where he lifted off: "On that day His feet will stand on the Mount of Olives, which faces Jerusalem on the east. The Mount of Olives will be split in half from east to west, forming a huge valley, so that half the mountain will move to the north and half to the south" (Zech. 14:4).

The angels had another goal in mind. They were doing more than reminding the disciples that Jesus would return as promised—they were applying a kick in the pants. It was time to stop gazing and get on with the task ahead.

And there is a lesson for us. As much as Jesus appreciates our prayers, praise, and worship, there remains a job to do. Using the gifts we have, we take what we have seen and know and share it with the world. We can almost hear the angels say, "Men of Phoenix, why do you stand looking up into heaven? You women of Miami . . . youth of Seattle . . . seniors of London . . ."

Faith has feet. The disciples had to leave that glorious place where the Savior went skyward. Jerusalem was a short distance away and with it the work of the gospel. So what did they do? They took the praise of the mountain to the city.

Jerusalem was just two miles away from Bethany. What is two miles from you?

Chapter 16

An Interrupted Journey

Last of all, as to one abnormally born,
He also appeared to me.
—1 CORINTHIANS 15:8

Your religion is no good. Does this shock you?

Let me add: religion is useless.

Sounds odd coming from a Christian, but I mean it. Religion is useless; worse, it can be counterproductive.

In an issue of *SBC Life,* published by the Southern Baptist Convention's Executive Committee, appeared a list of facts and insights drawn from Barna Research Group. Some of them struck me as especially important:

- Of adults who attend Christian church services, 41 percent are not born again. That's four out of ten of us.
- Religious teaching minimally affects people's moral choices. More powerful influences are personal outcome and minimizing conflict.

- Only 22 percent of Americans believe there is an absolute truth. This is in the country considered more Christian than any other.
- There is no difference in the divorce rate between Christians and non-Christians.
- Religion is becoming a function of convenience. By the end of the decade, fifty million Americans will seek to have their spiritual experiences through the Internet rather than church.
- After the September 11 terrorist attacks, religious activity surged. Two months later every spiritual indicator suggested things were back to preattack levels.[1]

Bottom line: Religion is no good. Spirituality is a different matter. Religion is something we do. Spirituality is something we are. They are not the same. Just ask Saul of Tarsus. No one epitomized the difference between religiosity and faith more than the man we know as the apostle Paul. Sometime after the ascension he had a close encounter of the Jesus kind that not only changed him but altered the future of Christianity and formed our Bible.

So Smart as to Be Stupid

Paul, then known as Saul, is first mentioned in the Bible attending a gruesome execution. A man named Stephen offended the religious leaders by his preaching. So angry were those who heard his message that they challenged him on every point but could not stand against Stephen's God-inspired response. Since they could not refute his teaching, they resorted to conspiracy, stating under oath they had heard Stephen blaspheme.

After a stirring sermon that left the blame of Christ's crucifixion on their shoulders, the men lost control. The Bible records it this way: "When they heard these things, they were enraged in their hearts and gnashed their teeth at him. But Stephen, filled by the Holy Spirit, gazed into heaven. He saw God's glory, with Jesus standing at the right hand of God, and he said, 'Look! I see the heavens opened and the Son of Man standing at the right hand of God!' Then they screamed at the top of their voices, stopped their ears, and rushed together against him. They threw him out of the city and began to stone him. And the witnesses laid their robes at the feet of a young man named Saul" (Acts 7:54–58).

Look at the descriptions: "enraged in their hearts," "gnashed their teeth," "screamed at the top of their voices." This was violence at its worst.

A mob of angry and cruel men hauled Stephen, one of the church's first deacons, out of the city and stoned him to death. We can almost see the twisted faces of the furious men as they encircle the deacon, cursing him. Then, in a deliberate fashion, they removed their outer robes so as not to hinder their throwing arms. Those robes they laid at the feet of a rising religious star, Saul of Tarsus.

Stephen died with a grace that is convicting to this day. As the stones struck him, bruising his body and breaking his bones, the first martyr called out, "Lord Jesus, receive my spirit!" Then kneeling, he prayed, "Lord, do not charge them with this sin!" (Acts 7:59–60).

Stephen then fell to the ground, battered to death.

Saul of Tarsus watched, approving of every stone hurled at the innocent man—and he thought God was pleased with him for doing so.

For Saul, this was just the beginning.

Saul gloried in persecution. Instead of being appalled at the violent (and illegal) act of stoning, Saul was inspired: "Saul agreed with putting him to death. On that day a severe persecution broke out against the church in Jerusalem, and all except the apostles were scattered throughout the land of Judea and Samaria. But devout men buried Stephen and mourned deeply over him. Saul, however, was ravaging the church, and he would enter house after house, drag off men and women, and put them in prison" (Acts 8:1–3).

The word "agreed" in this passage carries the idea of pleasure and gratification. We can almost imagine Saul thinking, *That's one less Christian.* Later Saul would admit to this crime using the same word (Acts 22:20).

The moment Stephen died, something evil was born. Instead of feeling guilt over the murder of an innocent man, those involved, especially Saul, began a "severe persecution." It came suddenly. It was vicious. One line tells us much: "Saul, however, was ravaging the church, and he would enter house after house, drag off men and women, and put them in prison" (v. 3).

What a terrifying sentence. Saul did more than bother the church, he "ravaged" it. The term (*elumaineto*) means to defile, ruin, even devastate. This is the only place in the New Testament the word is used. This was not a subtle persecution.

He forcibly entered houses, pulling people from their homes because they dared to be Christians. The early church met in homes, and it's likely Saul targeted these houses. Ironically, these Jews were acting like the Romans they so hated. There were no civil liberties, no due process of law.

Saul did something else astonishing. He dragged off "men and women, and put them in prison." The inclusion of women is surprising and shows the extent Saul was willing to go to end the growing church.

Driven by a legalism rooted in hatred, Saul pounded the early church, and it seemed no one could stop him. Saul was a man of violence, prejudice, and spiritless religious fervor. All he did, he did in the name of God. Hatred was his fuel—pure, hot, putrid hatred. His motto was simple: "Thou shalt believe as I do."

We are shocked at what the Nazis did to the Jews, what Stalin did to Armenians, what Serbs and Croats have done to each other, what Hutu and Tutsi have committed. Ironic, isn't it, that the man who wrote thirteen of the New Testament's twenty-seven books was just such a man.

Saul had an impressive résumé, and he used it to achieve his ends. Years later, after his conversion, Saul (now Paul) stood before an angry Jewish mob and defended himself with these words: "I am a Jewish man, born in Tarsus of Cilicia, but brought up in this city at the feet of Gamaliel, and educated according to the strict view of our patriarchal law. Being zealous for God, just as all of you are today, I persecuted this Way to the death, binding and putting both men and women in jail, as both the high priest and the whole council of elders can testify about me. Having received letters from them to the brothers, I was traveling to Damascus to bring those who were prisoners there to be punished in Jerusalem" (Acts 22:3–5).

He was a man of the "right" race (Jewish), born in a prestigious city (Tarsus) and lived in the "right" city (Jerusalem), had the "right" teacher (Gamaliel), lived the "right" life, and had the "right" zeal, which he expressed in persecution.

We could number Saul with the great enemies of the faith: Herod the Great, Herod Antipas, Caiaphas, the Pharisees, and Sadducees.

A Funny Thing Happened

Saul had become an irresistible force, a juggernaut of fury. With the power of the high priest, the ruling religious council of elders behind him, Saul was unstoppable.

Well, nearly unstoppable.

> Meanwhile Saul, still breathing threats and murder against the disciples of the Lord, went to the high priest and requested letters from him to the synagogues in Damascus, so that if he found any who belonged to the Way, either men or women, he might bring them as prisoners to Jerusalem. As he traveled and was nearing Damascus, a light from heaven suddenly flashed around him. Falling to the ground, he heard a voice saying to him, "Saul, Saul, why are you persecuting Me?"
>
> "Who are You, Lord?" he said.
>
> "I am Jesus, whom you are persecuting," He replied. "But get up and go into the city, and you will be told what you must do."

> The men who were traveling with him stood speechless, hearing the sound but seeing no one. Then Saul got up from the ground, and though his eyes were open, he could see nothing. So they took him by the hand and led him into Damascus. He was unable to see for three days, and did not eat or drink. (Acts 9:1–9)

Watching Saul in those early weeks of the persecution must have been frightening. As often happens in violent persecutions, things went from bad to worse. Luke, who would later travel with Paul, used phrases like "breathing threats" and "murder" to describe Saul's activity. If the last word seems like hyperbole, Paul would later admit he persecuted the church "to the death" (Acts 22:4).

When he felt that Jerusalem had been thoroughly purged, he expanded his borders to track down Christians in other towns like a religious bounty hunter.

Wildfires are common in certain terrains. Colorado, California, and other Western states have seen fire sweep across grasslands, leaving nothing but ashes behind. Wildfires have no sense of borders; they just wreak havoc. Saul wasn't much different.

Saul set his sights on the inland town of Damascus in the north. He gathered what papers he needed and started on his way, intent on filling Jerusalem jails with more Christians.

Along the way, Saul got a rude awakening. A light came from heaven and shone around Saul. He was in a hot, heavenly spotlight. Saul fell (very likely was knocked) to the ground. Although not specifically stated, his fall seemed tied to the light. Perhaps the light was intense enough to stun the persecutor.

No sooner than Saul hit the ground he heard a voice: "Saul, Saul, why are you persecuting Me?"

If Saul wasn't confused before, he was now. His first thoughts must have been, *I've persecuted scores of people. Which one are you?* Jesus made the question personal. Saul wasn't just persecuting the Christians, he was persecuting Christ.

In moments, there was an attitude change. "Who are You, Lord?" Saul asked. This was the same man who agreed with and watched the killing of Stephen. Now he was leveled to the ground and heard something he didn't understand.

Reality police shows on television are very popular. In many cases, the camera follows a policeman as he chases a criminal. When captured, the formerly tough guy turns polite, referring to the officers as "Sir." Once handcuffed, many change their tune. Saul decided a little courtesy might be useful.

Jesus gave Saul a taste of what the man had been dishing out. Saul was no longer in control, but a force greater than he could imagine had personally leveled him.

Then came the words. "I am Jesus, whom you are persecuting." No matter how hot the day, I'm certain a chill ran down Saul's spine and for several reasons.

First, Saul realized he was in big trouble. Second, he understood everything the Christians had been saying about a resurrected Jesus was true. Third, everything Saul previously believed was wrong. He may have believed he was on a mission for God, but he now knew that he had backed the wrong side.

Saul was told, "But get up and go into the city, and you will be told what you must do" (v. 6). The good news: He was going to live. The bad news: Saul was no longer in control.

He left Jerusalem to go to Damascus to spread the persecution and imprison Christians. Now he would go to Damascus as planned, but he would be led there by the hand.

Saul was blind.

For three days, he sat in darkness. While the busy streets of Damascus filled the air with their sounds, Saul could do nothing but wait and wait and wait. He also had time to think.

Then came the humbling hour.

Does This Count?

Before moving on, we need to ask a question: Did Saul see Jesus? Does this count as a resurrection appearance? After all, the light blinded Saul.

Years after this event, Paul stood before King Agrippa and gave an account of himself. His words added a few details to Luke's description of events:

> "At midday, while on the road, O king, I saw a light from heaven brighter than the sun, shining around me and those traveling with me. When we had all fallen to the ground, I heard a voice speaking to me in the Hebrew language, 'Saul, Saul, why are you persecuting Me? It is hard for you to kick against the goads.'

> "But I said, 'Who are You, Lord?'
>
> "And the Lord replied: 'I am Jesus, whom you are persecuting. But get up and stand on your feet. For I have *appeared to you for this purpose,* to appoint you as a servant and a witness of things you have seen, and of things in which I will appear to you. I will rescue you from the people and from the Gentiles, to whom I now send you, to open their eyes that they may turn from darkness to light and from the power of Satan to God, that they may receive forgiveness of sins and a share among those who are sanctified by faith in Me.'" (Acts 26:13–18)

Paul told us the event happened about midday, when the sun would be high in the sky. He also revealed that the light was "brighter than the sun," and it encompassed not only Saul but all those who traveled with him. They saw the light and heard something they couldn't understand. Only Saul heard the words, and what amazing words they were.

There, on that road to Damascus, Saul was confronted and commissioned. Often preachers like to say, "Jesus knocks at the door of your heart. He won't kick down the door. You have to open it to him." That wasn't true in Paul's case. Jesus didn't ask Saul if he now believed, if he had repented, if he understood his sin. Instead, Jesus issued commands and gave his purpose: Paul was to be a servant and a witness, and was being sent to the Gentiles.

Saul had been drafted.

Also in this passage is the promise of a postresurrection appearance. Just as Jesus told the disciples he would meet them on a certain mountain, Jesus promised to appear to Saul again. But before that would happen, Saul had to endure humbling.

In a single sentence, Jesus informed Saul that not only were his persecuting days over, but he was going to become one of the persecuted, so much so that Jesus would have to rescue him from the people (Jews) and the Gentiles (non-Jews).

A man named Ananias was recruited to be the instrument of a miracle. His job was to lay hands on a man whose mission had been to arrest Christians in Damascus—Christians like Ananias. The prey would minister to the hunter.

> Now in Damascus there was a disciple named Ananias. And the Lord said to him in a vision, "Ananias!"
>
> "Here I am, Lord!" he said.
>
> "Get up and go to the street called Straight," the Lord said to him, "to the house of Judas, and ask for a man from Tarsus named Saul, since he is praying there. In a vision he has seen a man named Ananias coming in and placing his hands on him so he may regain his sight."
>
> "Lord," Ananias answered, "I have heard from many people about this man, how much harm he has done to Your saints in Jerusalem. And he has authority here from the chief priests to arrest all who call on Your name."
>
> But the Lord said to him, "Go! For this man is My chosen instrument to carry My name before Gentiles, kings, and the sons of Israel. I will

> certainly show him how much he must suffer for My name!"
>
> So Ananias left and entered the house. Then he placed his hands on him and said, "Brother Saul, the Lord Jesus, who appeared to you on the road you were traveling, has sent me so you may regain your sight and be filled with the Holy Spirit."
>
> At once something like scales fell from his eyes, and he regained his sight. Then he got up and was baptized. And after taking some food, he regained his strength. (Acts 9:10–19)

This was the humbling hour and not just for Saul. Jesus sent a Christian to help Saul. In some ways, it was an odd mission. Jesus could have healed Saul without the help of any man. After all, it was he who blinded him in the first place. But he had other motives besides a healing of blind eyes. Imagine the psychological impact on both men. Had Jesus not intervened, Ananias would probably have been a victim of Saul. No doubt Saul had men such as Ananias in his sights. The humbling shoe was on the other foot as well. Saul, who hated all things Christian and any man associated with Christianity, was now at the mercy of the very ones he persecuted.

Saul's reputation had spread through the land, in a day with no radio or television. Word of mouth had reached the cities in the north and perhaps other lands, carried by Christians who had been driven from home and business, many of whom had friends and family in Jerusalem jails. Now Ananias received marching orders that chilled him to the marrow.

This is one of the most poignant events in all the New Testament. The powerful, influential, fearsome persecutor was cut down to a helpless blind man waiting for a Christian to set him free again.

Ananias was in a Jonah situation, called to minister to someone he feared. Unlike Jonah, who made every effort to thwart God's call on his life, Ananias hitched himself up and walked to the street named Straight to face the man who had done so much harm.

So Saul sat. So Saul waited in darkness. So Saul fasted and prayed. Then came Ananias's voice out of the darkness, "Brother Saul, the Lord Jesus, who appeared to you on the road you were traveling, has sent me so you may regain your sight and be filled with the Holy Spirit."

Scales fell from the persecutor's eyes, and his vision returned. The first thing he saw was the face of a man who, three days before, Saul would have loved to see dead—a man who now called him "Brother Saul." That man was now his first teacher.

Food brought him strength, healing brought him sight, and baptism brought him into the fellowship he had tried so hard to crush. How did such a man sleep at night, knowing that everything he believed was not only wrong but an affront to God? How did he rest, knowing that as he lay on his comfortable bed, scores, maybe hundreds, of Christians lay on the floor of a cell?

The years would push a different Saul on stage. His name would become Paul, and his goals would be the opposite of what they had been. All because Jesus confronted him on the Damascus road.

Paul saw the risen Christ more than once. Describing his change from persecutor to preacher, he wrote the following words to the church in Galatia:

> Now I want you to know, brothers, that the gospel preached by me is not based on a human point of view. For I did not receive it from a human source and I was not taught it, but it came by a revelation from Jesus Christ.
>
> For you have heard about my former way of life in Judaism: I persecuted God's church to an extreme degree and tried to destroy it; and I advanced in Judaism beyond many contemporaries among my people, because I was extremely zealous for the traditions of my ancestors. But when God, who from my mother's womb set me apart and called me by His grace, was pleased to reveal His Son in me, so that I could preach Him among the Gentiles, I did not immediately consult with anyone. I did not go up to Jerusalem to those who had become apostles before me; instead I went to Arabia and came back to Damascus. (Gal. 1:11–17)

"For I did not receive it from a human source," Paul said, "and I was not taught it, but it came by a revelation from Jesus Christ." *Revelation* means to lay bare, to unveil. Paul's teacher was none other than Jesus, who appeared to him a number of times.

When Paul did go back to Jerusalem sometime later, he was not welcome. Word of his conversion had spread, but it was difficult to separate rumor from fact. Fortunately, Jesus had a helper by the name of Barnabas selected to stand for Paul. "When he arrived in Jerusalem, he tried to associate with the disciples, but they were all afraid of him, since they did not believe he was a disciple. Barnabas, however, took him and brought him to the apostles and explained to them how, on the road, Saul had seen the Lord, and that He had talked to him, and how in Damascus he had spoken boldly in the name of Jesus" (Acts 9:26–27).

Did you catch the significant line? "Barnabas . . . explained to them how, on the road, Saul had seen the Lord." The account in Acts doesn't mention Saul seeing Jesus, but Paul's testimony was that he did lay eyes on the Savior before being blinded. In other words, the last image on Saul's retinas for three days was the face of Jesus.

Paul told of another time when Jesus appeared to him:

> "After I came back to Jerusalem and was praying in the temple complex, I went into a visionary state and saw Him telling me, 'Hurry and get out of Jerusalem quickly, because they will not accept your testimony about Me!'
>
> "But I said, 'Lord, they know that in synagogue after synagogue I had those who believed in You imprisoned and beaten. And when the blood of Your witness Stephen was being shed, I myself was standing by and approving, and I guarded the clothes of those who killed him.'
>
> "Then He said to me, 'Go, because I will send you far away to the Gentiles.'" (Acts 22:17–21)

In that case, Jesus himself brought the warning to Paul. It's important not to dismiss this appearance as merely a vision. Visions are very real for the person involved. Unlike a dream in which the recipient sees things happen, in a vision the visionary is a participant and experiences everything as physically as he would in daily life. The longest example of this is the book of Revelation.

Later in Paul's ministry, after an especially dangerous confrontation, Jesus appeared to Paul again: "The following night, the Lord stood by him and said, 'Have courage! For as you have testified about Me in Jerusalem, so you must also testify in Rome'" (Acts 23:11).

"The Lord stood by him." A magnificent phrase. Jesus has been standing by Christians on the front lines for many centuries.

Paul was an eyewitness to the resurrection of Christ. Not during the first forty days, but several times over the years. Each appearance was as real and as significant as those of the women, the disciples, and the five hundred.

So Impressed as to Change

The lasting effect of the postresurrection appearance to Saul was that one man was changed and his life changed that of millions. The antagonist became an apostle. He was a man shocked into change, and that change would impact the world for Christ like no other's.

He underwent a symbolic name change. A man of great ego was forced to see his real size. *Saul* means "desired"; *Paul* is from the Latin for "small" or "little."

When Paul faced his Savior, he was forced to face his

errors. What that did to his mind and emotions is beyond our imagination. He was granted a second chance, and he made use of it. His achievements are unrivaled. He was an instrument of miracles, made three missionary journeys, founded numerous churches, wrote much of the New Testament, took Christian theology to heights never again matched, and endured personal persecution, beatings, shipwreck, and danger—something he did gladly.

In the end, Paul became a magnificent tool in the hands of Jesus and lived to an old age. His life was never simple, and he fought not only the elements and persecution, but also false teachers who followed in his wake, corrupting what he shed sweat and tears to start. He spent much time in prison and finally died a martyr's death by beheading.

All of this because Jesus rewrote Paul's priorities. Hand-selected by Jesus, he was given a second chance and he did something with it.

We are all the beneficiaries of the second chance. The question is, what will we do with our new beginnings, our new opportunities?

Paul received several special visits from Jesus. Some think they might be more faithful if Jesus appeared to them. It is true that Paul was unique in this, but his calling was more challenging than that faced by any other man. To do what Jesus wanted him to do, he needed such visits. He paid for such special encounters with his sweat, blood, and ultimately his life.

On the Damascus road two thousand years ago, the man who would rock the world for Jesus was broken and reformed. And we are the beneficiaries of the remarkable event.

Part 3

Never the Same

"God has resurrected this Jesus.
We are all witnesses of this.
Therefore, since He has been exalted
to the right hand of God
and has received from the Father
the promised Holy Spirit,
He has poured out what you both see and hear."

—ACTS 2:32–33

Men and women disbelieve the Easter story
not because of the evidence but in spite of it.

—J. N. D. ANDERSON

Chapter 17

With the Greatest Confidence

Urban legends are popular. Thanks to the Internet, they spread quickly. An urban legend is a shocking or humorous story that while incredible has just enough truth to appear real. There are tales of a scuba diver inadvertently sucked into the water tank of a firefighting helicopter and dropped to his death on a forest fire. It's a tragic story. It is also false. The Christian community has its share of urban myths including stories about NASA computers proving Joshua's long day and accusations that Procter & Gamble is a satanic organization. Both are false.

For some reason, people often choose to believe nonsense even when the truth is clearly present. This reaches new heights with the Resurrection. Start a casual conversation with a group of unbelievers about the Resurrection, and soon bizarre theories come to the surface.

Let's face it. The Resurrection is hard to believe. After all, we're speaking of a man who endured horrible beating, cruel impalement, and heartbreaking death, then came back to life and appeared to scores of people. Doubt is understandable. But because something is hard to believe, it does not follow that it is false.

Early medical practitioners had trouble believing that creatures invisible to the eye could be responsible for infection and disease. In 1872, Pierre Pachet, professor of physiology at Toulouse said, "Louis Pasteur's theory of germs is ridiculous fiction." Today we call those germs bacteria and viruses.

Some things stretch the imagination too much. Tom Watson, chairman of IBM in 1943, said, "I think there is a world market for maybe five computers."

Naysayers abound, and the stories of their failed predictions are legendary. The Beatles were told guitar music was on the way out. Fred Smith was informed by his Yale University professor that his concept of overnight delivery was not feasible, but Federal Express was founded anyway. Alexander Graham Bell was told the telephone was impractical.

These are doubts about technology, society, and business, all of which pale in comparison with what people are asked to believe about the Resurrection. Still, the facts are there, and the Resurrection is beyond doubt to those who take the time to look at the evidence.

Yet, every few years someone publishes "proof" that the Resurrection never occurred. Most of these have the same credibility level as urban myths.

Doubters are not new; they can trace their philosophical lineage back to the first century. The apostle Paul addressed a batch of them in the Corinthian church:

> Now if Christ is preached as raised from the dead, how can some of you say, "There is no resurrection of the dead"? But if there is no resurrection of the dead, then Christ has not been raised; and if Christ has not been raised, then our preaching is without foundation, and so is your faith. In addition, we are found to be false witnesses about God, because we have testified about God that He raised up Christ—whom He did not raise up if in fact the dead are not raised. For if the dead are not raised, Christ has not been raised. And if Christ has not been raised, your faith is worthless; you are still in your sins. Therefore those who have fallen asleep in Christ have also perished. If we have placed our hope in Christ for this life only, we should be pitied more than anyone. (1 Cor. 15:12–19)

The Resurrection and the appearances of Christ were the center of apostolic preaching. Christian preaching is an empty thing without the Resurrection. So those doubters in the Corinthian church had heard the message time and time again, yet it rubbed their sensibilities the wrong way. Some may have accepted the resurrection of Christ but denied that the Christian will also be resurrected at Christ's coming.

The problem rests in an assumption made then and often made today: Christianity can exist without the Resurrection. In other words, the Resurrection is dispensable.

Paul didn't think so. He ticked off a short list of what the faith loses if there was no Resurrection:

- Preaching is without foundation.
- Faith is without foundation.
- We become false witnesses about God.
- Our faith is worthless.
- We are still in our sins.
- Those who have fallen asleep in Christ (died) have perished.
- We are to be pitied.

Quite a list.

On a hill in Athens, Paul preached his short but famous unknown god sermon. As usual, he included the resurrection of Christ. The response? A few believed, but most ridiculed him (Acts 17:32). Ridicule is the first response of doubters. Nothing has changed.

Those that don't ridicule do their best to explain away the Resurrection. They offer ideas that are more "reasonable." Ironically, the ideas are so contrived and lacking in historical integrity as to be ridiculous.

Despite the shaky nature of the theories, many have caught on.

Mostly Dead Theory

The 1987 movie *Princess Bride* has what must be one of the funniest lines in the movie business. The hero has been taken to Miracle Max (played by Billy Crystal) to be healed of his injuries. The hero's friends are concerned that they are too late and ask if he is dead. Max studies the lifeless form for a few moments then answers, "Well, it just so happens that your friend here is only mostly dead. There's a big difference between mostly dead and all dead."[1]

Mostly dead? How can someone be only mostly dead? As ridiculous as it sounds, the most popular theory used to dispel the Resurrection can be called the mostly dead theory. Usually it goes by the more formal title the swoon theory.

The idea was propagated through Hugh Schonfield's 1965 book *The Passover Plot.* In the widely read work, Schonfield suggested that Jesus contrived to be arrested, planned to be crucified, and did so knowing that he would be taken down before the Sabbath. Instead of dying on the cross, Jesus merely swooned—he passed out. Once in the cool tomb, he revived and made his way out of the sepulchre.[2]

There are several variations of this theme. One is that Jesus, with the full knowledge and help of the disciples, staged the execution. Another proposes that Jesus was revived by a doctor hidden in the tomb.

Other variations exist, but all assume that Jesus did not die. This theory doesn't work for many obvious reasons. This concept is so faulty it is difficult to know where to begin.

First, the theory requires that Jesus lied about his intentions. Would Jesus have spent three years teaching a moralistic gospel and go to the cross for his beliefs if it all hinged on a lie? The notion is contrary to everything Jesus taught and to his nature as revealed in his life and the lives of his disciples.

This plot would also mean the disciples were participants or were so foolish they were repeatedly deceived before and after the Resurrection.

Not only would Jesus have had to be a grand conspirator for the Passover plot to work, but he would have had to pretend to die. He would have needed to become an actor on the cross.

Furthermore, it would be necessary for the Roman guards—men who specialized in crucifixion—to have taken Jesus down before he died. The biblical text shows the extent the soldiers went to, to make certain the two thieves died before sundown—they broke their legs, hastening death. Jesus, they determined, was already dead. It is doubtful that men who went to such extremes to make certain that those crucified with Christ died would be so sloppy as to overlook Jesus' condition.

We should remember that Jesus was pummeled with fists and rod, scourged with a whip, and forced to carry the crossbeam to Calvary, a task he couldn't finish. Then he was nailed through hands and feet and left to suffer on the cross for six hours, and finally stabbed in the side. If the swoon theory is to be believed, we must also believe that Jesus overcame all that and was strong enough to recover in the tomb, move the rock, and walk past the guards.

In the burial chapter we discussed two men: Nicodemus and Joseph of Arimathea. If Jesus were alive, these two men would have known it. They wrapped Jesus' body, making it improbable that such a severely wounded man could have freed himself without help.

The passover plot/swoon theory starts off weak and deteriorates from there.

Twins Theory

As difficult to accept as the plot/swoon theory is, what Robert Greg Cavin of Cypress College offers is even more ludicrous. He suggests that Jesus had a twin whom he calls Hurome. In a nutshell, Jesus and his twin were separated soon after birth. Hurome arrived in Jerusalem in time to see his twin brother Jesus crucified. It seemed a good idea to him to take Jesus' place as Messiah. He, therefore, stole the body and picked up where Jesus left off.

William Lane Craig of the Talbot School of Theology calls this the *Dave* theory after the movie. (In the movie *Dave,* a presidential look-alike is pressured into masquerading as the recently deceased president.)[3]

Why doesn't this work? First, it requires there was a twin in the first place. Nowhere in the biblical text, extrabiblical texts, or history is found the mention of Jesus' twin. It would be something Mary and Joseph might have noticed.

For this to have even a shred of credibility, the New Testament must be gutted of its historical testimony. The Gospels not only relate the account of the crucifixion and resurrection but the unique nature of Jesus' birth, his miracles, his teaching, and much more.

Not only must there have been a twin for this theory to work, but he had to be a unique individual; for he arrived in Jerusalem, saw the tortured, battered body of Christ with a placard over his head that read "King of the Jews," and then considered it prudent to pick up where Jesus left off. It seems unlikely someone seeing the horrific, garish image would think it wise to try the same thing.

This, and other theories, require that we dismiss Jesus' prophecies about his death and resurrection. Actually, we have to dismiss much of the Bible.

Further, this bizarre concoction demands the disciples were gullible enough to be fooled by a twin. As the father of twins, I can say that no matter how much twins look alike, they have readily discernible distinctions, especially adult twins. And if not gullible enough to be fooled, then the disciples would have to have been participants in a fraud—a fraud for which they all suffered imprisonment, beatings, and martyrdom.

Hurome would have to have been a very clever man, for he had to, as an imposter new to the scene, know how Jesus spoke and what he taught, including the use of catch phrases and "reminder acts," like the breaking of bread with the two Emmaus disciples.

He had to be more than clever; he had to be powerful to work the postresurrection miracles that so impressed the disciples: walking into a closed room, miraculous catch of fish, appearing and disappearing before witnesses.

Lastly, this concept requires that Jesus' twin ascended into heaven before a band of Jesus' witnesses.

Supporters of this theory would quickly say, "None of those miracles happened either." If that is their belief, wouldn't it be more academically and intellectually ethical to say so? Why concoct such a nonsensical, groundless theory? Why suggest that Jesus had a twin? If it is an attempt to explain away the appearances of Christ, why not just call those fabrications as well?

Big Cover-Up Theory

We love a good conspiracy tale, so it's not unusual that some folk believe the Resurrection is nothing more than a fine-tuned fabrication—fiction contrived for personal gain.

The story goes like this: After Jesus' death and burial, the disciples got together and devised a scheme that would make the world think that Jesus rose from the dead as he said he would.

Thinking that the last three years of ministry were better than fishing or tax collecting, they conspired to keep things going. They stole the body and buried it elsewhere, then told people they'd seen Jesus alive again and witnessed him rise into heaven forty days later. Now they're the leaders, and the fame that had been Jesus' would now be theirs.

This doesn't work either. If this theory were true, it must be the dumbest idea in history. It is hard to imagine the disciples saying, "Let's start an organization that will infuriate our Jewish brethren and irritate the Romans." They had just witnessed what happened to Jesus. Why would they want to take the same abuse for something that wasn't true?

Again, it would require the disciples—every one of them—to be liars. It also means these men were ready to die for a lie. It lacks a reasonable motivation, and the price would far outweigh the personal gains.

Men and women will die for the truth, but very few will willingly suffer for something they know to be a lie. Even if we can stretch our imaginations enough to believe several disciples would condescend to perpetrate such a fraud, it is impossible to believe all of them would participate.

This is the earliest of the Resurrection debunking theories. Matthew shows us its origins: "As they were on their way, some of the guard came into the city and reported to the chief priests everything that had happened. After the priests had assembled with the elders and agreed on a plan, they gave the soldiers a large sum of money and told them, 'Say this, "His disciples came during the night and stole Him while we were sleeping." If this reaches the governor's ears, we will deal with him and keep you out of trouble.' So they took the money and did as they were instructed. And this story has been spread among Jewish people to this day" (Matt. 28:11–15).

That contrived concept would spread worldwide and last through the centuries.

The Gullible Gentlemen of Galilee

A favorite way to attack the Resurrection is to attack the witnesses in general and the disciples specifically. One popular theory is that the disciples were the victims of mass hypnosis. So eager were they to believe that Jesus would rise as he said he would, they began—as a group—to "see" him.

A variation of this idea suggests that Jesus selected people who had highly suggestible personalities whose imaginations would lead them to see things, hear things, and touch things that were not there.

As with the previous theories, this one has problems. First, while it might be possible to trick a group of people once or twice, it would be difficult to do so repeatedly over a period of forty days.

The disciples not only saw Jesus, they touched him, ate with him, and listened to him. Some of these sightings involved groups like the women, the disciples, the five hundred, but others were one on one (Mary Magdalene, Peter, and James).

The appearances of Christ occur at different times in the day, in different locales (from Jerusalem to Galilee), and with a varying mix of people. One can imagine *a* mass hallucination, but a *dozen* is beyond the boundaries of credibility.

Full Confidence

Two millennia after the event, contemporary Christians can state their belief in the resurrection and postresurrection appearances of Christ without bowing their heads in shame. No argument exists that has put the smallest dent in the armor of truth.

The Resurrection and appearances are reasonable—the result of reason. While there are those who wish to cast the believer as a gullible supporter of myths, the evidence shows otherwise. The ridiculous theories put forth to explain away the Resurrection are easily seen for what they are: desperate attempts to avoid the supernatural intervention of God.

The Resurrection is a historical fact replete with eyewitnesses. The fact that the church meets on Sunday is just one piece of evidence the early believers took the Resurrection literally.

There will always be critics. Detractors plagued Jesus during his ministry and the disciples in the early church and will continue to do so until Jesus returns.

The Resurrection requires an ability to believe in the supernatural work of God. For those who dismiss such things, no amount of evidence or logic will serve as proof.

While we should show patience with those who have doubts—remember, the Resurrection is a difficult concept—we need not be embarrassed by the biblical account.

Chapter 18

The New Jesus

No matter how much we know about the Resurrection, it remains a mystery. Questions arise faster than we can nail down answers. This doesn't indicate a problem with the Resurrection, but it does show that we have limited information.

Many questions swirl around Jesus' mysterious actions during the forty days of his appearances. On the one hand, it is clear Jesus made these appearances, but he did so in ways very different from his days of ministry.

It was the same Jesus; it was a different Jesus.

Those who have studied the appearances of Christ debate the nature of the risen Savior's body. At one moment, Jesus seemed as physical as the day he died; in the next moment he seemed incorporeal. The debate has spanned centuries.

That Jesus rose from the dead bodily should never be questioned. That truth is the very heart of the Resurrection. If Jesus did not rise bodily, where is the victory over death?

When Jesus appeared, he did so in the same body that went to the cross and was sealed in the tomb.

But some things changed.

The Physics of Being Physical

What did Jesus look like? No one knows. "Nowhere does the New Testament give us a description of the physical features of Jesus of Nazareth. The writers are preoccupied with his character, his action, and his teaching. Nor does the situation change in the resurrection narratives even though Jesus is alive from the dead in an immortal bodily form."[1]

There have been hundreds of artist renderings of Jesus, but not one of them is based on observation or description. The New Testament writers who, under the inspiration of the Holy Spirit, penned the New Testament never spoke of his height, skin tone, length of hair, body weight, or any other aspect of his appearance. As Harris noted above, the writers were concerned with Jesus' character and teaching. Appearance didn't matter.

Still, that Jesus was a physical being and not some spiritual hologram is clear from his actions. Through his ministry, he touched, ate, drank, walked, spoke, reclined at the table, was pressed by crowds, was touched by others, and ultimately whipped, pummeled, forced to carry a heavy wood crossbeam, and had nails driven through very real hands.

Although the first-century Gnostics argued against the physicality of Jesus, they did so to promote an agenda. They separated Jesus the man from Jesus the Christ. They viewed the human body as an evil thing; therefore, the Christ could not have a body. The Gnostics' day came and went. The apostles argued persuasively against them, pressing home the point that Jesus possessed a very real body.

John argued the point in his first epistle:

> What was from the beginning,
> what we have heard,
> what we have seen with our eyes,
> what we have observed,
> and have touched with our hands,
> concerning the Word of life—
> that life was revealed,
> and we have seen it
> and we testify and declare to you
> the eternal life that was with the Father
> and was revealed to us—
> what we have seen and heard
> we also declare to you,
> so that you may have fellowship along with us;
> and indeed our fellowship is with the Father
> and with His Son Jesus Christ.
> We are writing these things
> so that our joy may be complete.
> (1 John 1:1–4)

John emphasized the physical senses: we heard, we saw, we examined, and we touched. Sight, sound, and touch. John wanted his reader to know that Jesus was not a mirage and that as his disciple, he had laid hands on Jesus and perceived him with his other senses.

Eight hundred years ago, Thomas Aquinas argued this point again and did so with several points.[2] First, Jesus appeared in a physical body, but not just any physical body—it was the same one that went to the tomb. He did not get a new body (although we will see that he used that body in some astounding new ways).

Second, Aquinas mentioned the "nutritive life." Jesus ate and drank after the Resurrection. Whether or not he needed to is another matter.

Third was the "sensitive life." Jesus was responsive to questions; greeted those he appeared to; saw, heard, and understood conversation; and was sensitive to the emotions of those around him.

Fourth, as physical and human as Jesus was after the Resurrection, there was a "divine nature" seen by his working of miracles and his ascension.

No one questions Jesus' physical nature before the Resurrection, but it becomes an issue for some afterward. Yet, every activity Jesus engaged in is further proof he was appearing in his physical body.

Physics is involved. The eyewitnesses never described Jesus as hovering above the ground. Before and after his resurrection, he walked on solid earth; and when he did so, he put one foot in front of the other. To walk, a person must press one foot against the solid earth. Force is exerted and motion achieved. The risen Jesus left footprints.

To speak, vocal cords must vibrate air; tongue and mouth are used to adjust sounds; and words come out. Of course, it is much more complicated than that, but the point is that Jesus spoke the way humans speak. Granted, some might argue that God spoke from a burning bush and from thin air above the ark of the covenant. Certainly, Jesus could have communicated any way he chose, but the way he chose was through a physical body.

Here is where we sometimes stumble in our understanding. Jesus still had his body. Sometimes people think Jesus took on a body he was using for a time. That is a faulty assumption. Jesus returned bodily as he ascended bodily. Jesus was the "firstfruits" of the resurrection (1 Cor. 15:20), and believers are to be the rest of the harvest (1 Cor. 15:23). We as believers are to be raised from the dead bodily just as Christ was. For our resurrection to make sense, Jesus must have been raised bodily.

Beyond Physics

All that being said, Jesus did do some things beyond the realm of normal physics. Let's call these "supraphysical acts." *Supra* is a prefix that means "above" or "beyond." Just like supernatural means "above nature" (that is, what we believe to be normal in nature), supraphysical means "above the physical."

I coin this term to avoid other terms that seem to confuse the issue or say more than is intended. Some like to speak of Jesus' spiritual body; but the term implies a body that is not physical, and we want to avoid that implication.

Several times during the forty days of his appearances (and after that with Stephen and then Paul), Jesus defied the basic laws of physics. Of course, Jesus did that many times when he performed miracles. Stilling the storm, converting water into wine, raising the dead—all go against standard physics. In some ways, breaking the laws of science is the very definition of a miracle.

We saw these events as we studied each of the appearances so they're not new to us, but we haven't looked at the ramifications.

Borrowing (with some adaptation) from theologians like John Walvoord, we can categorize the supraphysical events.

First, transportation was no barrier. Jesus appeared at the tomb outside Jerusalem, in Jerusalem, on a road leading from the city to a small town, on a mountain in Galilee, by the seashore, then at the Mount of Olives a short distance from Jerusalem. On two occasions Jesus was seen walking, first on the road to Emmaus, then from Jerusalem to the Mount of Olives. In every other case, Jesus merely appeared on the scene with no explanation of how he arrived.[3]

It appears he could move from place to place at will, unencumbered by space and time. And others experienced similar movement. Acts 8:26–40 tells of Philip, one of the original deacons. Philip received divine instruction to approach an Ethiopian eunuch who was traveling home from Jerusalem. He did so, and the man, after hearing the gospel, received Christ and sought baptism. Philip immersed the new convert, then the strange happened: "When they came up out of the water, the Spirit of the Lord carried Philip away, and the eunuch did not see him any longer. But he went on his way rejoicing. Philip appeared in Azotus, and passing through, he was evangelizing all the towns until he came to Caesarea" (Acts 8:39–40). Philip was "spirited away" and appeared in a town twenty-five miles north of Gaza.[4]

Another event of physics-defying travel is recorded in

John: "When evening came, His disciples went down to the sea, got into a boat, and started across the sea to Capernaum. Darkness had already set in, but Jesus had not yet come to them. Then a high wind arose, and the sea began to churn. After they had rowed about three or four miles, they saw Jesus walking on the sea. He was coming near the boat, and they were afraid. But He said to them, 'It is I. Don't be afraid!' Then they were willing to take Him on board, and at once the boat was at the shore where they were heading" (6:16–21).

So gripping is the drama that we often overlook the line "at once the boat was on the shore where they were heading." Mark's account reveals that the boat was in the "middle of the sea" (6:47). The Sea of Galilee is eight miles across at its widest point, so the boat moved in an instant to the shore four miles away.

Space and time have never been barriers to Jesus, not during his earthly ministry, and they certainly presented no problems after his resurrection.

A second category of Jesus' supraphysical acts has to do with the manner in which he arrived. Jesus appeared behind closed doors. The implication is that he materialized before the eyes of the disciples, throwing them into a panic. Since they first believed "they were seeing a ghost" (Luke 24:37), we can assume that Jesus didn't open the doors before entering. Interestingly, when the disciples saw Jesus walk on the water, they assumed they were seeing a ghost (Mark 6:49). Looking back with our 20–20 hindsight, we wonder how they could think such things; but had we been there, our response would have been the same. Just as space and time were no barrier to Jesus, neither was the material world.

Locked doors could not keep him from being somewhere he wanted to be.

A third area of the supraphysical was Jesus' ability to appear and disappear at will. In the Upper Room, he appeared at will; at the home of the Emmaus disciples, Jesus vanished before their eyes after doing very physical things such as breaking bread and reclining at the table. It is one thing to see such things in a science fiction movie but a very different thing to see it at the dinner table.

One of the amazing qualities in these accounts is how little detail the Scripture gives. Appearing and disappearing at will, defying gravity at the Ascension and the other supraphysical acts demand details, but little is given. Perhaps this is to keep our attention on the One who was raised. Nonetheless, Jesus proved he was physical in every respect and yet transcended our definition of physical as well.

Encounter	Jesus' Arrival	Jesus' Departure	Physical Act	Supraphysical Act
Mary Magdalene	Behind Mary, unnoticed	Unknown	Spoke, was touched	–
The Women	As they left the tomb; no details	Unknown	Met, spoke, was touched	–
Peter	Unknown	Unknown	Spoke	–
The Emmaus Two	Approached, previously unnoticed	Vanished	Walked, talked, lifted bread, sat	Sudden appearance, vanishing; opened the minds of the two
The Ten Plus the Two	Sudden appearance	Unknown	Displayed his hands and feet, ate fish	Appeared in locked room (assumed), opened their minds

Encounter	Jesus' Arrival	Jesus' Departure	Physical Act	Supraphysical Act
The Eleven (Thomas)	Sudden appearance in locked room	Unknown	Spoke, offered his body for examination	—
The 500	Unknown	Unknown	Was seen	—
The Seven	Appears on shore (disciples at sea)		Spoke, prepared food, presumably ate	Had fish and fire going
James	Unknown	Unknown	Spoke	—
The Eleven (Ascension)	Unknown	Ascended in full view and mid-blessing	Walked, spoke	Ascended
Paul, Damascus Road	Sudden and dramatic, light from heaven	Unknown	Spoke	After death and resurrection

Where's the Glory?

Sometimes people describe these appearances as Jesus appearing in his glorified body, but were they? Matthew recorded an event in which the disciples got their first look at Christ's glory:

> After six days Jesus took Peter, James, and his brother John, and led them up on a high mountain by themselves. He was transformed in front of them, and His face shone like the sun. Even His clothes became as white as the light. Suddenly, Moses and Elijah appeared to them, talking with Him.

> Then Peter said to Jesus, "Lord, it's good for us to be here! If You want, I will make three tabernacles here: one for You, one for Moses, and one for Elijah."
>
> While he was still speaking, suddenly a bright cloud covered them, and a voice from the cloud said:
>
> This is My beloved Son.
> I take delight in Him.
> Listen to Him!
>
> When the disciples heard it, they fell facedown and were terrified.
>
> Then Jesus came up, touched them, and said, "Get up; don't be afraid." When they looked up they saw no one except Him—Jesus alone.
> (17:1–7)

Three disciples—Peter, James, and John—were selected to see something no one else saw. Taking the three men to a high mountain, Jesus was transfigured (from *metamorphoo*), changed, as they stood by watching. That change included a change in Jesus' face, which "shone like the sun," and his clothing, which "became as white as the light."

Here they catch a glimpse of what Jesus would become, a transfigured body with the white glow of divinity. For a few moments, the earthly drabness fell away, and Jesus was seen in his full glory.

Joining him were two special people: Moses and Elijah. To have seen Moses must have been amazing. Moses had died and been buried, yet he stood on this mountain, having a conversation with Jesus. Also, there is one of two men who never died: Elijah (Enoch was the other—Gen. 5:24; Heb. 11:5).

There is a lot of material here to grab our attention, but for the purpose of this chapter we want to focus on the changed Jesus. His face (and presumably his body) was altered and so were his clothes.

Jesus appeared in great light that rivaled the sun. This is his glory, yet we see none of it during the period of resurrection appearances. Jesus did not appear in his glorified body until after the Ascension. Stephen the martyr and Saul the persecutor saw Jesus after his ascension and witnessed him in his glory.

Why not? Why not appear to the disciples and others as he did on the Mount of Transfiguration?

The question lies in a common misconception. Too often we see the death and resurrection of Jesus as the end of something, when it is really the continuation of his work on earth. The Crucifixion did not put the period at the end of Christ's earthly ministry—the Ascension did. There was more ministry to accomplish first. Jesus demonstrated his return to life and work by appearing, teaching, giving final orders, then ascending to heaven.

By appearing the way he did, Jesus demonstrated the meaning and power of the Resurrection, something that will occur to all believers. "He will transform the body of our humble condition into the likeness of His glorious body, by the power that enables Him to subject everything to Himself" (Phil. 3:21).

Jesus proved the point.

Next, it will be our turn.

How Did He Do It?

It's human nature to want to know all the secrets. I once sat with hundreds of others as we watched the premier magician David Copperfield work his "magic." A spectacular showman, Copperfield soon had us all in his grasp. Things appeared and disappeared, including him. With every trick, every sleight of hand, and stage prestidigitation I asked myself, "How did he do that?" Then I set about trying to figure it out. I wanted to know.

When we read of Jesus appearing in locked rooms and disappearing in front of the watchful eyes of the disciples, we immediately want to know how he did it. No matter how great our desire to know, the best we can do is theorize.

Recent theories from the world of physics lend an interesting idea. More and more we are hearing of the multidimensional nature of the cosmos. Scientists are saying there exist at least eleven dimensions. Those are the *proven* dimensions.[5] Such a concept is hard to grasp. I have heard it said that only people with doctorates in physics and young children can understand anything beyond our four dimensions.

We operate in a world with limits. God created the universe in such a way as to support human life. That requires at least three special dimensions and one dimension of time. It is beyond the scope of this book to discuss such things in detail, but there is a point to be made.

What is meant by a dimension? Imagine you're on an airplane winging through the air. Your forward travel is one dimension. If the pilot banks left or right, that's a second dimension. The aircraft can go up and down, so there's the third dimension. These represent the three spatial dimensions.

Another way to view this is to stand in the middle of a room. You can take a step forward or to the side or jump in the air. Three dimensions.

The fourth dimension is time. Everything happens in the course of time.

Those are the four dimensions that we deal with daily, but research is showing that there are at least eleven dimensions, something nearly impossible to describe. We have no basis or experience to help us visualize such a universe, yet it is nonetheless there.

What does this have to do with the resurrection appearances of Christ? It might help us understand how Jesus did some of the things he did. This is not an attempt to dilute the miraculous nature of Jesus' actions. On the contrary, it heightens our appreciation of what he has done and can do.

Ross wrote, "Jesus Christ's incarnation and resurrection represent the most dramatic and significant expressions of God's extra-dimensional capacities."[6]

It appears Jesus was able to overcome great distances, appear and disappear at will, and the many other things he did because he was no longer limited to the four dimensions in which we dwell. If that is true, the incarnation of Jesus was even more dramatic and praiseworthy. It means he left an existence of many dimensions and confined himself to just a few—our few.

To understand this, imagine losing one of our dimensions. Let's say that we can move only forward and to the sides—two dimensions. Life would be dramatically changed. (Actually, it would cease to work at all.) We would be beings with breadth and width but no height.

Now reverse that. Imagine a two-dimensional being trying to comprehend our three-dimensional world. It would be difficult, perhaps impossible. We face the same challenge in trying to comprehend a world with seven more dimensions than ours.

Jesus, in his resurrected body and soon to be glorified body, was able to move in realms we cannot.

Does this explain it all? Not by a long shot, but it does give us something to consider.

One day, we shall know.

Chapter 19

Who Did the Raising?

Andy Rooney of *60 Minutes* fame is said to have quipped, "There's nothing people like better than being asked an easy question. For some reason, we're flattered when a stranger asks us where Maple Street is in our hometown and we can tell him."

There's something to that. Easy questions, however, do not always mean easy answers. Who did the raising? In other words, who brought Jesus back to life?

Seems easy enough, doesn't it? For the most part it is, but there is a twist in the tale. First, the obvious.

God Raised Him

After Jesus' ascension, the disciples waited in Jerusalem just as he ordered them to do. It was about a ten-day wait until Pentecost, a Jewish holiday celebrated fifty days after Passover. Jerusalem was again abuzz with people, including pilgrims who had traveled from various lands.

Also known as the Festival of Harvest (Exod. 23:16) and the day of firstfruits (Num. 28:26), the feast day was held seven weeks after the second day of Passover. It was one of the three obligatory feast days.

For forty days after his resurrection, Jesus made appearances, then ascended into heaven. The next ten days the disciples waited for the promised power (Acts 1:4–8). As pledged, the Holy Spirit descended, and the formerly meek disciples spilled out onto the crowded streets of Jerusalem, proclaiming the gospel. Peter delivered his first sermon, and in that message he quoted an Old Testament passage. He said:

> "*God raised Him up,* ending the pains of death, because it was not possible for Him to be held by it. For David says of Him:
>
> I saw the Lord ever before me;
> because He is at my right hand,
> I will not be shaken.
> Therefore my heart was glad,
> and my tongue rejoiced.
> Moreover my flesh will rest in hope,
> because You will not leave my soul in Hades,
> or allow Your Holy One to see decay.
> You have revealed the paths of life to me;
> You will fill me with gladness in Your
> presence.
>
> "Brothers, I can confidently speak to you about the patriarch David: he is both dead and buried, and his tomb is with us to this day. Since he was a

> prophet, he knew that God had sworn an oath to him to seat one of his descendants on his throne. Seeing this in advance, he spoke concerning the resurrection of the Messiah:
>
> He was not left in Hades,
> and His flesh did not experience decay.
>
> "*God has resurrected this Jesus.* We are all witnesses of this." (Acts 2:24–32)

Twice, Peter stated that God raised Jesus. In fact, this is the preponderance of evidence in the New Testament. Almost every time the resurrection event is mentioned, it was God who accomplished it and Jesus is referred to in the passive—that is, it was happening to him.

Peter said it again in another sermon: "But you denied the Holy and Righteous One, and asked to have a murderer given to you. And you killed the source of life, *whom God raised from the dead*; we are witnesses of this" (Acts 3:14–15).

It wasn't just Peter's opinion. Paul said the same in one of his messages: "*But God raised Him from the dead,* and He appeared for many days to those who came up with Him from Galilee to Jerusalem, who are now His witnesses to the people" (Acts 13:30–31). He also stated in his letter to the Romans, "*Christ was raised from the dead by the glory of the Father*" (6:4b), and in his epistle to the Ephesians, "He demonstrated [this power] in the Messiah *by raising Him from the dead* and seating Him at His right hand in the heavens" (1:20).

That should pretty much settle it, but a closer look shows Jesus said he would raise himself.

He Raised Himself

Early in Jesus' ministry, he made a dramatic move by driving out the money changers and other business interests from the temple courtyard. This didn't go over well, and the merchant and religious leaders wanted to know by what authority he did these things. His answer was cryptic, surprising and revealing for us.

> So the Jews replied to Him, "What sign of authority will You show us for doing these things?"
>
> Jesus answered, "Destroy this sanctuary, and I will raise it up in three days."
>
> Therefore the Jews said, "This sanctuary took 46 years to build, and will You raise it up in three days?"
>
> But He was speaking about the sanctuary of His body. So when He was raised from the dead, His disciples remembered that He had said this. And they believed the Scripture and the statement Jesus had made. (John 2:18–22)

Looking back on the event, we see that Jesus was speaking of the Resurrection, but those of his day didn't get the message. John even put in a little explanation. What makes this passage so interesting is Jesus' statement, "I will raise it up in three days." If taken as is, then Jesus is the one responsible for raising himself.

But then comes John's insert, "So when He was raised from the dead . . ." It's in the passive, meaning someone else resurrected Jesus.

Later, Jesus said something similar: "This is why the Father loves Me, because I am laying down My life so I may take it up again. No one takes it from Me, but I lay it down on My own. I have the right to lay it down, and *I have the right to take it up again.* I have received this command from My Father" (John 10:17–18).

Again, Jesus spoke of laying down his life and taking it up again, but he also mentioned he had received a command of his Father. Both are involved.

There's a third person to consider.

Holy Spirit

There is a passage that indicates the Holy Spirit was also involved: "And if the Spirit of Him who raised Jesus from the dead lives in you, then He who raised Christ from the dead will also bring your mortal bodies to life through His Spirit who lives in you" (Rom. 8:11).

We do not know the mechanism used to bring Jesus back to life after three days in the tomb. There had been great physical damage to his body, decay had begun, cell death was in process, then came the unexplained miracles that reversed all that.

God raised Jesus from the dead, but it can also be said that Jesus raised himself and the Holy Spirit was the agent in the miracle. In other words, the Trinity was fully involved in the Resurrection as it was in Creation.

Although we don't know the process, we do know the outcome, and it has changed eternity.

Chapter 20

The Difference It Makes

We've followed Jesus from the Garden of Gethsemane and tried to get a sense of the early agony that drove him to the ground. From there we saw the brutality inflicted by his enemies. We then followed the dark path to the crucifixion point and saw the kind of death Jesus died. We've looked in the tomb before and after the Resurrection and then carefully examined the biblical text regarding the resurrection appearances of Christ and the effect these had on those who witnessed him. It's been a long journey.

But now we sit two thousand years removed from the event. Since his death and resurrection, electricity has been discovered, men have gone to the moon, space has been explored by robot craft, advances have been made in medicine, the average life span has increased by decades, and computers have connected the four corners of the world.

The religious scene has seen the rise of hundreds of belief systems, and the number of people intent on destroying the credibility of Christianity has expanded.

So what are twenty-first-century people to do? How are we to gaze back across misty centuries, and what do we do with the information we discover?

Do those great events of long ago make a practical difference to us? The answer is yes. The Resurrection altered many things, including things we do every week.

When We Meet

Most Christian churches meet on Sunday. Many Christians attend worship services with no idea why they're meeting on Sunday rather than another day.

The Jews of Jesus' day (as well as contemporary Jews) worshiped on the Sabbath. The weekly Sabbath day was not Sunday but began at sundown on Friday and continued until sundown Saturday. It was a day to be kept holy, and the order to keep it special is one of the Ten Commandments: "Remember to dedicate the Sabbath day: You are to labor six days and do all your work, but the seventh day is a Sabbath to the LORD your God. You must not do any work—you, your son or daughter, your male or female slave, your livestock, or the foreigner who is within your gates. For the LORD made the heavens and the earth, the sea, and everything in them in six days; then He rested on the seventh day. Therefore the LORD blessed the Sabbath day and declared it holy" (Exod. 20:8–11).

It was an important matter, not one to be taken lightly. Several of the criticisms leveled at Jesus were his refusal to conform to the additional laws and requirements added to the commandment. To some of his religious enemies, Jesus and his disciples were Sabbath breakers (Matt. 12:1–8; Luke 6:9–10; John 5:5–10).

It was on the Sabbath that the New Testament-era Jews rested and went to synagogue. It was a practice deeply ingrained in them. For the Christian that all changed after the Resurrection.

At first, the apostles continued to go to the temple (Acts 3:1), as much to preach the new gospel as to continue previous behavior; but soon the church began to meet on the first day of the week—Sunday (Acts 20:7; 1 Cor. 16:2).

The reason for the change was the Resurrection. Jesus rose from the grave on a Sunday morning. Over time, the local church—usually congregations that met in homes—would gather to sing, share the Lord's Supper, and worship on Sundays.

Each Sunday gathering was a celebration of the Resurrection. No matter the size of the group or the sermon topic, the fact that believers gathered on Sunday was testimony to their belief in the bodily resurrection of Christ.

While this might seem a simple change, it is much more. The entire Jewish culture surrounding the church was fixated on a set of religious laws that began with God and to which men added unnecessary requirements. The early Jewish Christians had been brought up with those laws drummed into their ears. Year after year, they followed the same routine. Now a change was afoot. They were stepping away from their previous behavior and that of their parents, grandparents, and uncounted generations.

Today we give no thought to attending church on Sunday, but for the new believer in the first century, it was a life-changing decision and a public proclamation. Why bother, if the Resurrection weren't true? One of the great proofs for the Resurrection is the early and continued choice of the church to meet on Sundays. The distance between the seventh day and the first day of the week was long, but the early Christians made the journey anyway.

The fact that there is a church to attend on Sunday is proof of the Resurrection. The early church was evangelistic in the face of persecution and rejection. Believers lost homes and jobs, and later many lost their lives in horrible fashion. What prompted men and women to suffer ridicule and in later years face crucifixion, burning, stoning, and death by wild animals? Only a belief in the Resurrection could garner such commitment. "Only such definite proof of the deity of Christ would have given the church the convincing power that it needed in the gospel witness."[1]

Josh McDowell asked a convincing question: "Do you believe for a moment that the early church could have survived for a week in its hostile surroundings if Jesus Christ had not been raised from the dead? The resurrection of its founder was preached within a few minutes' walk of Joseph's [of Arimathea] tomb. As a result of the first sermon, immediately after arguing for a risen Christ, three thousand believed. Shortly thereafter, five thousand more believed."[2]

Isn't it interesting that none of the three thousand who responded to Peter's first sermon felt it necessary to stroll over to the tomb and look for the body of Jesus? I suspect they already knew the truth. Peter's sermon forced them to focus on what they needed to do with that knowledge (Acts 2:41).

The church has endured much over the centuries—attacks from without and weakness from within—but it continues its work into the twenty-first century. Missionaries still leave home for foreign fields, scholars still study and teach, preachers still preach, worshipers still worship. The core of the church remains, thanks to the Resurrection.

The Way We Grieve

Nothing is so painful or so enduring as the loss of someone we love. Whether expected or sudden, the hole left is impossible to fill. Time levels the ups and downs we feel, but those who have buried a family member know the wound never completely heals.

The first-century Christians were no different. They faced death as frequently as we do (perhaps more) and felt the same soul-stabbing pain. Paul tried to comfort them in one of his letters. He wrote to those in Thessalonica, people who were concerned their dead loved ones would miss out on the coming of Christ.

> We do not want you to be uninformed, brothers, concerning those who are asleep, so that you will not grieve like the rest, who have no hope. Since we believe that Jesus died and rose again, in the same way God will bring with Him those who have fallen asleep through Jesus. For we say this to you by a revelation from the Lord: We who are still alive at the Lord's coming will certainly have no advantage over those who have fallen asleep.

> For the Lord Himself will descend from heaven with a shout, with the archangel's voice, and with the trumpet of God, and the dead in Christ will rise first. Then we who are still alive will be caught up together with them in the clouds to meet the Lord in the air; and so we will always be with the Lord. Therefore encourage one another with these words. (1 Thess. 4:13–18)

Paul revealed that the Resurrection changed the way we look at death and the manner in which we grieve. Ever the scholar, Paul appealed to the reader's intellect: "We do not want you to be uniformed, brothers, concerning those who are asleep, so that you will not grieve like the rest, who have no hope" (v. 13). The solution to their sadness, Paul concluded, was the Resurrection and all that it means.

The first clue to Paul's thinking is his use of the word *asleep* for death. Terms reveal a person's thinking, and Paul's opinion spilled out in his word choice: He saw death differently than the rest of the world. Jesus used the euphemism twice (Mark 5:39; John 11:11), and Peter once (2 Pet. 3:4), but Paul worked it into his writing about ten times. For Paul, it was the best expression for those who die in faith.

Rather than giving them a literary pat on the back and cooing, "There, there, it will be all right," Paul directed their attention back to the Resurrection: "Since we believe that Jesus died and rose again" (1 Thess. 4:14a). For him (and for us) it is the logical place to start. Who understands more about death and life than Jesus?

What Paul wanted them to do was put their belief in Jesus' resurrection to work in the present life. Those who have gone on before us will return when Jesus comes again. Then there is this bombshell: "We who are still alive at the Lord's coming will certainly have no advantage over those who have fallen asleep" (v. 15).

"Advantage" here is from the Greek term (*phthano*) for precede, to take precedence over. In other words, the dead are not at a disadvantage when it comes to the return of Christ. In a sense, they are a step ahead of those who remain.

Paul then described the resurrection of believers. Those who have died return with Christ; those who remain alive at the time of Christ's coming are caught up to meet him in the air.

All of this (and so much more) he based on the fact that Jesus died and rose from the dead. His message to the Thessalonians is simple, "Don't fret. God who raised Jesus has not forgotten your loved ones or you." He then called them to encourage one another with those words.

Ever since, the Christian view of death has been different from the rest of the world's.

Around AD 125, a Greek named Aristeides wrote to a friend, trying to explain the unusual spread of a new religion called Christianity. In his letter he wrote, "If any righteous among the Christians passes from this world, they rejoice and offer thanks to God, and they accompany his body with songs and thanksgiving as if he were setting out from one place to another nearby."[3]

Christians shed as many tears as unbelievers, but those tears come with the sense of personal loss, not because we think our loved one has ceased to exist. The Resurrection has changed our view of this life and the next, as well as our view of the event called death.

The Way We Die

For some, it is easier to face their own death than the passing of someone they love. Even so, staring death in the eye is never easy. Yet Christ's resurrection changed the way the early church, and every believer since, looked at death. When Paul faced his own death, he was conflicted: "For me, living is Christ and dying is gain. Now if I live on in the flesh, this means fruitful work for me; and I don't know which one I should choose. I am pressured by both. I have the desire to depart and be with Christ—which is far better—but to remain in the flesh is more necessary for you" (Phil. 1:21–24).

For him, going was better than staying. Notice how he viewed death: To Paul, it was departing one place to be with Christ—the risen Christ. This isn't the kind of statement a man makes who doesn't believe in the Resurrection. Most likely, Paul knew he would die a martyr's death. He had seen the deaths of his fellow apostles and church leaders. He would be no different.

Still, the thought of death brought him joy, not despair. He even mentioned the pressure he felt. His heart was already in heaven, but his work was still on earth.

When other men backed away from the fact of death, Paul embraced it. Why? Because he knew death was nothing more than a gateway to a life promised by Jesus. Randy Alcorn has studied the concept and biblical revelation of heaven for years. He noted, "Tragically, most people do not find their joy in Christ and Heaven. In fact, many people find no joy at all when they think about Heaven."[4]

Paul could not be numbered with those souls. His mind was anchored on heaven because that was where Christ was—

the risen Christ. This world held nothing for him except the gospel he so faithfully preached. He had friends and loved ones, but they would one day join him in heaven.

The Resurrection appearances remind us that life continues on after death. Because of Jesus, death has no more hold on us than it did on him. Consequently, Christians view their own deaths differently.

During my pastor days, I met many who teetered on death's threshold. Some had endured lingering illness; others had come to their last days quickly. Often they spoke of the joy that awaited them. Family members shed tears when they breathed their last, but their first words were of the joys of heaven.

Before his death, before his resurrection, Jesus spoke of what he would accomplish on our behalf: "Your heart must not be troubled. Believe in God; believe also in Me. In My Father's house are many dwelling places; if not, I would have told you. I am going away to prepare a place for you. If I go away and prepare a place for you, I will come back and receive you to Myself, so that where I am you may be also. You know the way where I am going" (John 14:1–4).

This statement came as a command. "Stop allowing your heart to be troubled," we might say. Notice Jesus' logic: "You believe in God, then believe in me." Once that was established, he reminded the disciples a place in heaven awaited each of them, prepared by Jesus himself. Then he promised to return for the purpose of receiving us to himself.

This can only be achieved by a resurrected Savior. A powerful religious teacher can't do it. A kindhearted leader can't do it. Only God in the flesh, dead and raised, could achieve that future for us.

During our healthy years, few look forward to death. We were created to enjoy the act of living, but death comes to us all. No one gets out of this life alive (except those alive when Jesus returns). We can face the inevitable with the clear understanding that Jesus paved the way. His resurrection is the proof of our eternal life and future resurrection.

As a writer, I'm impressed by the epitaph of Benjamin Franklin, who spent much of his youth and adult life as a printer:

> Like the cover of an old book,
> Its contents torn out,
> And stripped of its lettering and guilding,
> Lies here food for worms.
> But the work shall not be lost
> For it will (as he believes)
> Appear once more,
> In a new and more elegant edition,
> Revised and corrected by the Author.

Benjamin Franklin was a complicated man with diverse interests, but toward the end of his life he understood that God the Author of lives has more planned for us.

The Way We Relate to Jesus

"If we are searching for the center point of Christian experience and testimony, we find it here," Thomas Oden wrote. "Only if the Lord lives now is it possible to have a personal meeting with him. The resurrection, therefore, should not be seen only as an idea or past event but as that which permits an experience of present personal encounter with the living Lord."[5]

It comes down to this: If Jesus did not rise from the dead, then there is no one with which to have a life-giving relationship. At best, we have a hero, a teacher, and a great philosopher; and while those things are noble themselves, we need most of all a Savior. Living on the Friday side of the tomb doesn't cut it; we must exist on the Sunday side, the raised-from-the-dead-now-and-forever-living side of the tomb.

One of the unique qualities of the Christian faith is that it is based on the mind-boggling concept that a person can have a relationship with the Creator. Not just a god-out-there theology but a vital, thriving relationship. Christians don't see God as distant; they don't see Jesus as a historical figure. Jesus is a present-tense Savior. Every other faith looks back in time, but Christians look back and look forward, all for the same purpose: to please Christ today. We are a three-tense people: past, present, future. They are not separate items but shades of the whole. None of us living today can literally stand at the foot of the cross, yet Christians stand in that shadow every day.

We cannot have a relationship with the dead. The Resurrection makes it possible for us to connect with Jesus the living. It is no accident that Jesus made numerous appearances. In each one, he brought about a change and shaped the future of an individual and his church, but each appearance also showed Christ's desire for continued fellowship.

Jesus could have exited the cold tomb and immediately ascended into heaven, but he didn't. Why? To remain in contact with his followers over forty days required a reason and a plan. Certainly, seeing the risen Christ was more convincing than seeing an empty tomb. But could there be more?

I think there is. Jesus could have made one appearance to a few hundred and left it at that. Instead, he not only manifested himself, but he sought out key individuals and met their needs.

He reversed Mary Magdalene's sorrow into joy and converted her from mourner to the first human to herald the truth about Christ. Jesus joined the two Emmaus disciples on the road and dealt with their discouragement. With Peter, it was reconciliation; with James, reunion; with Thomas, assurance; with the disciples, it was the Great Commission; and with Paul, it was correction and salvation.

Today, Jesus changes lives because of his resurrection. When we come to Jesus, we do so understanding who he is and what he's done: "This is the message of faith that we proclaim: if you confess with your mouth, 'Jesus is Lord,' and believe in your heart that God raised Him from the dead, you will be saved. With the heart one believes, resulting in righteousness, and with the mouth one confesses, resulting in salvation" (Rom. 10:8b–10).

This verse, well known but often overlooked, is the formula of faith:

confessing Christ as Lord + believing in the resurrection = salvation

That's how important the Resurrection was to Paul and the early church. It was an indispensable factor in faith.

The Lord's Supper and Baptism

Christ left two ordinances for the church to practice through the centuries: the Lord's Supper and baptism. The Lord's Supper is a reenactment of Christ's death, of his shed blood and broken body.

So central is the death and Resurrection to church life that it is a regular part of worship. Some churches celebrate the Supper (Eucharist) weekly while others only a few times a year. In either case, the congregation is being reminded of Jesus' suffering and death.

Baptism shows the other side of the tomb. Countless times over the years, I've had the pleasure to immerse many new believers. Each time I did, I spoke the same words: "In obedience to the command of our Lord and Savior Jesus Christ, I baptize you my brother/sister in the name of the Father, the Son, and the Holy Spirit. Buried with Christ in baptism, raised to walk in newness of life."

When explaining baptism to children, I often described the event as a stage play in which we show the world that we believe Jesus lived, died, and rose again.

In American Sign Language used by millions of deaf individuals, the sign for baptism is similar to that for death. In the latter the signer holds her hands out, separated by a few inches and palms facing each other. The hands are turned to the left until they are parallel and flat to the floor. The sign for baptism is the same except the hands immediately return to their original position—life, death, then life again.

Every believer's baptism is a portrayal of the church's and the new believer's belief in the bodily resurrection of Christ.

> Therefore we were buried with Him by baptism into death, in order that, just as Christ was raised from the dead by the glory of the Father, so we too may walk in a new way of life. For if we have been joined with Him in the likeness of His death, we will certainly also be in the likeness of His resurrection. (Rom. 6:4–5)
>
> Having been buried with Him in baptism, you were also raised with Him through faith in the working of God, who raised Him from the dead. (Col. 2:12)

Over and over again, the New Testament shows us how important the Resurrection is to church life.

Without it, there would be no church.

Chapter 21

An Under-this-world Appearance

We should consider one other appearance. To do so, we need to venture into a little understood world beyond our own. So far we have seen the postresurrection appearances of Christ that occurred during the forty-day period between his resurrection and ascension. We've also examined the postascension appearances to Paul and mentioned the "visionary" sightings by Stephen and John in Revelation. But there appears to be at least one more close encounter recorded in the Bible.

Unfortunately, as with Jesus' appearance to James, we have little to go on. Still, the fascinating passage is in the Bible, and its presence is no accident.

We Are Not Alone

While I was growing up, one of my favorite books was *We Are Not Alone.* Written in 1964 by Walter Sullivan, then science editor for the *New York Times,* the book examined the current thinking and research by scientists to find intelligent life on other planets.[1] I devoured other books, including less credible works on UFOs, secret civilizations living at the center of the planet, and similar topics. I was fascinated with the idea that other civilizations were still to be discovered. Science fiction became a mainstay for me. Little did I know then that my hunger for such things would be satisfied by the Bible and in a far more reasonable and credible manner.

Even a cursory reading of the Scripture reveals a world beyond what we humans experience daily. The Bible mentions angels, demons, and other creatures, without apology. Angels are mentioned more than three hundred times in the Bible. They are shown as intelligent, powerful, and as much alive as anyone we're likely to meet in the course of a normal day.

Some of the most fascinating (and admittedly puzzling) passages deal with nonhuman beings. King David wrote:

> Praise the LORD,
> [all] His angels of great strength,
> who do His word,
> obedient to His command.
> (Ps. 103:20)

Evil beings called demons and unclean spirits plagued many and were subject to the commands of Jesus and later the apostles.

The biblical view is humans are not alone and never have been. From Genesis to Revelation, angelic beings make significant appearances and are mentioned in thirty-four of the Bible's sixty-six books. These beings are not what most people envision. The world of art has led us to think of angels as chubby, fat-cheeked babies with wings. We even call babies "cute little cherubs." The Bible says angels are able to work in their realm and ours. They always appear as men and are referred to in the masculine.

They are created beings as old as Creation itself. Teaching the believers at Colossae, Paul wrote,

> [B]ecause by Him everything was created,
> in heaven and on earth, the *visible and the invisible,*
> whether thrones or dominions or rulers or authorities—
> all things have been created through Him and for Him. (Col. 1:16)

"Visible and invisible"—human pride makes it difficult for some to believe there can be intelligent beings other than humans and that there are realms unseen by us. Nonetheless, the Bible makes it clear we are not alone.

What does this have to do with postresurrection appearances of Christ? Because Jesus made a showing to those beyond our normal realm.

A Surprise Visit

Peter wrote these provocative words. Take a close look at them:

> For Christ also *suffered* for sins once for all,
> the righteous for the unrighteous,
> that He might bring you to God,
> after *being put to death* in the fleshly realm
> but *made alive* in the spiritual realm.
>
> In that state *He also went* and *made a proclamation to the spirits in prison* who in the past were disobedient, when God patiently waited in the days of Noah while an ark was being prepared; in it, a few—that is, eight people—were saved through water. Baptism, which corresponds to this, now saves you (not the removal of the filth of the flesh, but the pledge of a good conscience toward God) *through the resurrection of Jesus Christ. Now that He has gone into heaven,* He is at God's right hand, with angels, authorities, and powers subjected to Him. (1 Pet. 3:18–22)

The book of 1 Peter was written to Christians scattered by persecution. It is a work of encouragement and a call for perseverance in a time of great loss and constant uncertainty. On several occasions, Peter reminded readers of the Resurrection (1:3, 21 and twice in this passage).

Peter mentioned that Christ suffered, died, and was "made alive." This sets the context for what follows: "In that state He also went and made a proclamation to the spirits in prison" (v. 19a).

Every few words bring new questions:

"In that state": What state?

"He also went": Went where? Went when? Why did he go?

"Made proclamation": What kind of proclamation? What was said?

"To the spirits in prison": What spirits? What prison? Why were they in prison?

And there are no simple answers. When teaching at my church, I often reminded the congregation that knowledge should be divided into three categories: (1) that which I know is true; (2) that which I suspect to be true; and (3) that about which I don't have a clue. This passage has been debated for centuries and after the best minds in Bible and theology have hashed it all over, we still don't know exactly what Peter had in mind. Here's what I suspect is the case.

Since the passage is bracketed by mentions of the Resurrection, the context of these verses must center on that event. Peter stated that Jesus suffered, was put to death "in the fleshly realm and made alive in the spiritual realm." He then continued his thoughts with the connecting words, "in that state." What state was he in? The resurrected state is the only suitable answer.

A word of caution here. There is a common misconception that spiritual means noncorporeal, that creatures like angels do not have bodies. Granted, their bodies differ from ours, but they are not without substance. Just one example: When Peter was in prison (one of many times), he was freed by an angel who struck Peter on the side to wake him (Acts 12:7). The angel was solid enough to jar Peter out of a sound sleep. Other Bible passages indicate that angels have solid bodies.

When Peter commented that Jesus was made alive "in the spiritual realm," he did not mean to say that Jesus' resurrection was anything other than physical. The contrast is this: Men put him to death, and God raised him from the dead. And then as we've seen, his resurrected body was not confined to our spatial dimensions. Like the angels, he could appear and disappear, but Jesus was as physical after the resurrection as any one of us.

It was in his resurrected state that Jesus "went and made proclamation to the spirits in prison." The word *proclamation* comes from the words *to preach* or *to herald* (*kerusso*) and is used more than sixty times in the New Testament. It is the same word Jesus used in Matthew 24:14: "This good news of the kingdom will be proclaimed in all the world as a testimony to all nations. And then the end will come."

Another interesting phrase Peter used is "the spirits." As Kenneth Wuest and others noted, this phrase is never used for human beings.[2] These spirits are described as having been disobedient in the past "when God patiently waited in the days of Noah while an ark was being prepared."

It is here that most of us pull up short. Peter wasn't discussing any spirits but those disobedient ones during the days of Noah and prior to the Flood. To understand this we have to look at something else Peter wrote: "For if God didn't spare the angels who sinned, but threw them down into Tartarus and delivered them to be kept in chains of darkness until judgment" (2 Pet. 2:4).

In Peter's second book, he battled with false teachers who troubled the early church with false doctrine. In doing so, he called up three Old Testament examples of God's judgment. All of them are from the book of Genesis: (1) sinning angels (6:1–4), (2) the Flood of Noah (6:9–8:22), and (3) Sodom and Gomorrah (19:1–29).

Peter taught that those sinning angels were thrown

into Tartarus. This is the only place in the Bible Tartarus is mentioned, and most translations render it "hell." This is an unfortunate translation because it confuses two distinct places. Hell is a place of future punishment. For the sinning angels, Tartarus is a place of present imprisonment.

What is Tartarus? The name is used in other Greek literature as a gloomy place for evil people. In the New Testament it is the special prison for certain unrighteous angels. These are the same angels Jude spoke of: "He has kept, with eternal chains in darkness for the judgment of the great day, angels who did not keep their own position but deserted their proper dwelling" (Jude 6). The eternal chains in darkness must certainly be Tartarus.

If we have accurately examined these verses, it appears that Jesus, after his resurrection, went to Tartarus and proclaimed something to the imprisoned spirits there. Of course, that leads to the next natural question: What did he proclaim and why?

We're not told, but there might be a clue back in Genesis: "Noah was a righteous man, blameless among his contemporaries; Noah walked with God" (6:9b). "Blameless" is from a Hebrew word (*taamiym*) that means without spot, and it has been suggested the text is saying Noah was unpolluted by the rampant intermarrying of the sons of God (angels) and the daughters of men. Their offspring, the Nephilim, were unique in size and power.[3]

People like Chuck Missler have suggested that this mixing led to the pollution of the human genetics, hence the need for the Flood.[4] For 120 years Noah preached as he built the ark, but not a single individual saw the light. Apparently the intermarrying led to great violence with murder being routine. Only Noah and his family survived the Flood and in the process created a clean genetic slate. We are all descendents of Noah—and so was Jesus.

Another attention-grabbing phrase of Peter's is, "Baptism, which corresponds to this [the Flood and the death it brought], now saves you (not the removal of the filth of the flesh, but the pledge of a good conscience toward God) through the resurrection of Jesus Christ" (1 Pet. 3:21). He mentioned the removal of the filth of the flesh. By context we must assume that Peter was still thinking of the world right before the Flood and the filth (spot, contamination, dirt) of the flesh.

What did Jesus announce to those spirits in Tartarus? Was he offering them a second chance? Doubtful. There is no biblical evidence that fallen angels get a second chance. If they do, it hasn't been revealed to us.

What then? The 1 Peter 3 passage doesn't claim that Jesus evangelized, only that he heralded, proclaimed, preached some news. It might be that Jesus was there to prove the point. Their plan to destroy the bloodline didn't work; he had come, taught, died, and been raised from the dead. Victory was God's.

Could Jesus have made another proclamation? Of course. All we truly know is that Jesus made a proclamation to the spirits in prison and that these spirits are most likely the sons of God mentioned in Genesis 6.

For now we have far more questions than answers, and proper biblical interpretation does not allow us free speculation. Still, Peter gave us a glimpse of this mysterious resurrection appearance of Christ.

Chapter 22

Can This Be True?

In the late '70s a college friend attended a large, prestigious seminary. He had worked hard to get there. He had studied the Bible, preached when given the opportunity, and looked forward to serving God as pastor of a local church. He finished his four years of college and felt prepared for the rigors of three years of seminary. What could be better than being in an environment centered on the study of the Bible?

He was in for a surprise.

Many seminaries at that time were embroiled in controversy. Liberalism had spread its tentacles into many theological schools. Pressured by the need to conform to contemporary humanistic scholarship, many professors were leaving behind traditional teaching structured on biblical revelation and adopting philosophies labeled with such names as "German rationalism."

Before long, professors, under the cloak of "academic freedom," were teaching my friend that things he held to be true were false and nothing more than fabrications: The virgin birth was biologically impossible; life and the universe were the result of billions of years of chance happenings; Moses didn't write the first five books of the Old Testament because Moses couldn't write; the New Testament was not written by the authors whose names it bears; and Jesus didn't really rise from the dead.

He described to me the day he sat in class as the professor approached the doctrine of the Resurrection. After introductory remarks, the instructor gazed hard over the students. "You don't really believe in a resuscitated corpse, do you?"

It was a rhetorical inquiry asked in such a way as to make anyone who answered yes seem foolish.

Christians are asked to believe the impossible and in a day of pragmatism and denial, that task of belief becomes all the more difficult.

A resuscitated corpse? It was reduced to that. Two thousand years of unquestioned belief now dismissed with a sneer.

A resuscitated corpse? Is that what we're asked to believe? That two millennia ago Jesus died, was buried, and three days following his death, was raised back to life? Impossible. Beyond the realm of science and nature.

Yet, it is nonetheless true. It is the fact that the Resurrection is impossible and beyond the realm of science and nature that gives it its power. It is a unique event central to Christianity. Without it, the church becomes a social club.

Believing the Impossible

"You don't believe in a resuscitated corpse, do you?"

The words shocked the class and stunned my friend. They were new to him, and they landed hot on his heart. That professor wasn't the first one to throw doubt on the bodily resurrection of Christ, and he won't be the last.

The Resurrection is a demanding thing. You either believe it or you don't. In fairness, when we ask people to believe that Jesus was dead then was raised back to full, undiminished, enhanced life, we ask them to stretch the bounds of credibility. Our culture has lost the art of believing the unbelievable, of knowing that God can and has broken the laws of physics (as we know them) and that he had a right to—after all, he wrote those laws.

For some, it is too difficult a task to think that God could ever do something they cannot explain. Gerd Lüdemann is one such scholar. In a debate with William Lane Craig, he said, "Anybody who says that he [Jesus] rose from the dead is faced with another problem. . . . Namely, if you say that Jesus rose from the dead biologically, you would have to presuppose that a decaying corpse—which is already cold and without blood in its brain—could be made alive again. I think this is nonsense."[1]

Professor Lüdemann doesn't believe in the resuscitated corpse of Jesus.

He is not alone. The biology of the Resurrection makes it difficult for some to accept. It's common to hear men rail against miracles—"Defies the laws of physics" or "Doesn't agree with what we know about biology and chemistry."

And it's not just "them against us" thinking. More and more Christians are stepping away from some basic doctrines of the church. George Barna is noted for his consistent and in-depth look at trends associated with the church. A few years ago, he noted, "Large proportions of the lay leaders in Christian churches hold a range of unbiblical religious views regarding the holiness of Christ, the reality of Satan, the existence of the Holy Spirit, the reality of the resurrection, and the means to salvation."[2]

He's not speaking of people outside of church but lay leaders: Sunday school teachers, deacons, trustees, and board members. Even those brought up in the church stumble over the idea that Jesus could have died, been buried, then raised to life.

If Barna's observation is true, then a substantial portion of those who gather in church on Easter Sunday, do so with no real belief in what they're celebrating. The songs, the cantatas, the prayers, and the sermon are a sham. Author and pastor George MacDonald pulled no punches when he wrote,

> If Christ is not risen, we have nothing to believe. Everything hangs on that. Jesus would be a liar if he's not risen. He said he would rise. The Bible is a joke because it's filled with things that never happened.
>
> If Christ is not risen, let's send the people home, lay off the staff, lock up the building and give away the keys. I'll pack up my books and burn them. But we're all here because Christ is risen. Everything hangs on that. If Christ is not

> risen, Christianity is a colossal waste of time. Believe in what? Trust in what? Trust a god who's dead? Pray to a Savior whose body was eaten by dogs? Is that what we're doing? I don't think so.[3]

Does that sound like hyperbole? Was MacDonald an over-the-top fanatic? Hardly. I know many pastors would follow MacDonald's example. Without the Resurrection the church is a house of cards in a hurricane; but with it, it is a powerhouse geared to continue to change the world.

Can the contemporary mind believe in a resuscitated corpse? Or have we reached a point in history where belief in the impossible is . . . impossible?

Still, millions believe, and these believers are not buffoons. From every walk of life and every level of education come those who find no shame in saying, "Count me among the believers." Scientists, businessfolk, mathematicians, medical professionals, writers, artists, performers, carpenters, laborers—young and old have placed mind, heart, and faith in a brilliant moment two thousand years ago.

The Twenty-First-Century Mind and a First-Century Truth

We've come a long way in the last two millennia. The fastest a person could travel in Jesus' day was by chariot. Today we give no thought to flying at hundreds of miles an hour thirty-five thousand feet above earth. In Jesus' day the average working man lived thirty to forty years. Today we barely react to someone who turns one hundred. In the first century, appendicitis or an abscessed tooth could be deadly, and children died frequently. Today we have scores of antibiotics, antivirals, and machines like the CAT scan that can peer inside our bodies without shedding a drop of blood.

Technology has changed society and the way we do things, but it has not changed the basic human heart or mind. We have become rationalists and empiricists who demand proof for almost everything. Nothing wrong in that. The Resurrection makes more sense than most things, and the Christian need not fear a rational examination of the facts.

Such an examination has only verified the truth. Pamela Binnings Ewen, an attorney, did a detailed analysis of the Resurrection with the goal of proving a legal case could be made in defense of the event. Her book *Faith on Trial* lays out a well-reasoned case.[4]

In school, I was one of those children who gravitated toward the sciences. I loved astronomy and for many years thought that would be my career. It didn't happen, but my love for life and physical sciences has not faded. For a time, I was a science major in college. In high school and college I learned the scientific method and to think in a logical manner. Ironically, that training improved my Bible study and my faith. Many are not so fortunate. Year after year they are subjected to the truth of science and the superstition of everything else.

We have become a people who demand facts—or at least say we do. It's the way the Western mind thinks. The twenty-first-century mind hungers for proof.

Or is that true?

The Resurrection and the subsequent appearances appeal not only to the heart but to the rational mind. Those who have the biggest problem with the Resurrection are generally those who have studied it the least, or prefer not to face the conclusions of a risen Savior.

Why Bother?

The Resurrection is either the greatest moment in history or the greatest fraud ever perpetrated. In either case, it is worthy of study; but, believing as I do that the Resurrection is a fact, not a fable, I conclude it is worth our time because it is the event that threw open heaven's doors. It is proof of Jesus' claims and the example of what will happen to every believer.

As stated in the introduction, this is not a book defending the Resurrection. That has been done many times and by people better able to do so than I. This is a book about the personal aspects of Jesus' rise from the grave.

Jesus did not rise in a vacuum. He made appearances—purposeful, planned, appearances to change lives. Each appearance is a lesson for the witness and those who follow. This is not a bigfoot sighting in which a hunter or camper sees something in the distance he can't explain. Jesus' appearances were never chance encounters. They were personal, close, and done with a purpose.

Why bother? Because he bothered.

The great Scottish preacher who became the chaplain to the U.S. Senate, Peter Marshall, once exclaimed in a sermon, "Let us never live another day as if he were dead!"[5]

Why bother? Because his continued life is our eternal life. Unlike followers of any other religion, Christians follow a Savior who is alive, not entombed.

There will always be those, like my friend's professor, who will wag a finger our way and ask in a condescending voice, "Surely you don't believe in a resuscitated corpse, do you?"

Their voices might be intimidating and laced with scorn, but the answer for me and millions of others remains, "Yeah, I do."

Notes

Chapter 2: In Despair's Garden

1. Dallas Theological Seminary, *The Bible Knowledge Commentary: New Testament: An Exposition of the Scriptures,* eds. John F. Walvoord and Roy B. Zuck (Wheaton, IL: Victor Books, 1983–85), 269.

2. The apostle Paul called Luke the "beloved physician" (Col. 4:14).

3. www.ncbi.nlm.nih.gov/entrez/query.fcgi?cmd=Retrieve&db=pubmed&dopt=Abstract&list_uids=8982961.

Chapter 3: The Death Jesus Died

1. The young man mentioned in this passage was not named, but many scholars believe it was Mark. It is also believed that Mark's family may have owned the Upper Room where Jesus instituted the Lord's Supper and the enclosed area known as the Garden of Gethsemane.

2. Flavius Josephus, *The Antiquities of the Jews* 18.3.2.

3. Greek, Latin, Syriac, Armenian, and others.

4. Eusebius, *The Epistle of the Church in Smyrna,* chapter 2.

Chapter 4: From Wood Cross to Stone Tomb

1. Many translations have one hundred pounds. The word translated "pounds" is the Greek *litra* that represents about twelve ounces, not the sixteen-ounce pound. The actual weight of material brought by Nicodemus was close to seventy-five American pounds.

2. It is assumed that Joseph, her husband, died while Jesus was still young. He was seen in the account of twelve-year-old Jesus in the temple (Luke 2:41–50) but was never mentioned again.

3. Dallas Theological Seminary, *The Bible Knowledge Commentary: New Testament: An Exposition of the Scriptures,* eds. John F. Walvoord and Roy B. Zuck (Wheaton, IL: Victor Books, 1983–85), 341.

Chapter 5: The Enigmatic Tomb

1. Matthew 20:19; Mark 9:9, 14:28; John 2:19–22.
2. Numbers 19:11–13.
3. Job 9:6; Psalm 18:7, 60:2, 68:7–8, 114:7; Isaiah 13:13; Hebrews 12:26 are some examples.

Chapter 6: Encounter with Mary

1. The other five were Mary the mother of Jesus; Mary of Bethany, sister to Lazarus and Martha; Mary, mother of Mark and sister to Barnabas; Mary wife of Cleopas; and Mary, the fellow worker in Rome (Rom. 16:6).
2. Gospel of Philip, 50. This work, which exists only in fragments, was probably penned in the third century.
3. Gospel of Thomas, 114. The Gospel of Thomas is a Gnostic work containing the so-called secret sayings of Jesus. It was written sometime during the second century, long after the New Testament.

Chapter 7: The Women Came First

1. Pliny the Younger, *Letters* 10.96–97.

Chapter 9: On the Road with Jesus

1. Lee Strobel, *The Case for Christ* (Grand Rapids, MI: Zondervan, 1998), 237.
2. Flavius Josephus, *Wars* IV.1.3.

Chapter 10: The Unexpected Guest

1. This is assumed for purposes of illustration.
2. Kenneth S. Wuest, *The New Testament, An Expanded Translation* (Grand Rapids, MI: Eerdmans, 1961).

Chapter 11: The Odd Man Out

1. Gerald Ford, *A Time to Heal* (New York: Harper & Row, 1979), 289.
2. Edwin A. Blum, quoted in Dallas Theological Seminary, *The Bible Knowledge Commentary: An Exposition of the Scriptures,* John F. Walvoord and Roy B. Zuck, eds. (Wheaton, IL: Victor Books, 1983–1985), 344.

Chapter 12: Mountaintop Experience

1. See Matthew 14:21 and 15:38 as examples.
2. A. T. Robertson, *Word Pictures in the New Testament,* vols. 5 and 6 (Nashville, TN: Broadman Press, 1932, 1933; Bellingham, WA: Logos Research Systems, 1997).

Chapter 14: A Family Visit

1. Eusebius, *The History of the Church,* 7.19.
2. Flavius Josephus, *The Antiquities of the Jews* 20.9.1 (Peabody, MA: Hendrickson, 1997).

Chapter 15: The Big Exit

1. Quoted at the PBS Web site for the program *From Jesus to Christ,* www.pbs.org/wgbh/pages/frontline/shows/religion/jesus/jefferson.html.

Chapter 16: An Interrupted Journey

1. "2001: The Year's Most Intriguing Finds," *SBC Life,* June/July 2002.

Chapter 17: With the Greatest Confidence

1. *The Princess Bride,* a film script by William Goldman.
2. Hugh J. Schonfield, *The Passover Plot: A New Interpretation of the Life and Death of Jesus* (New York: Bernard Geis Associates, 1965).
3. William Craig vs. Robert Greg Cavin, "Dead or Alive? A Debate on the Resurrection of Jesus," Simon Greenleaf University.

Chapter 18: The New Jesus

1. Murray J. Harris, *From Grave to Glory* (Grand Rapids, MI: Zondervan, 1990), 139.
2. St. Thomas Aquinas, *Summa Theologica,* part 3, question 54, article 1.
3. John F. Walvoord, *Jesus Christ Our Lord* (Chicago: Moody, 1969), 203–04.
4. Craig S. Keener, *The IVP Bible Background Commentary: New Testament* (Downers Grove, IL: InterVarsity Press, 1993), Acts 8:40.
5. Hugh Ross, *Beyond the Cosmos* (Colorado Springs, CO: NavPress, 1996), 13.
6. Ibid., 49.

Chapter 20: The Difference It Makes

1. John F. Walvoord, *Jesus Christ Our Lord* (Chicago: Moody, 1969), 200.

2. Josh McDowell, *The Resurrection Factor* (San Bernardino, CA: Here's Life Publishers, 1981), 107.

3. Aristeides, *Apology,* XV.

4. Randy Alcorn, *Heaven* (Wheaton, IL: Tyndale, 2004), 5.

5. *This We Believe,* John H. Armstrong, John K. Akers, John Woodbridge, general editors (Grand Rapids, Zondervan, 2000), 113.

Chapter 21: An Under-this-world Appearance

1. See Walter Sullivan, *We Are Not Alone: The Search for Intelligent Life on Other Worlds* (McGraw-Hill, 1964).

2. Kenneth S. Wuest, *Wuest's Word Studies from the Greek New Testament: For the English Reader* (Grand Rapids, MI: Eerdmans, 1997, 1984).

3. Some argue that the sons of God could not be angels who had sexual relations with human women because Jesus said angels "neither marry nor are given in marriage" (Matt. 22:30), but Jesus was not speaking of *capability* but of *practice.*

4. Chuck Missler, further source details unknown at publication time.

Chapter 22: Can This Be True?

1. Paul Copan and Ronald K. Tacelli, eds., *Jesus' Resurrection: Fact or Figment?* (Downers Grove, IL: InterVarsity, 2000), 45.

2. George Barna, *The Barna Update,* "The Year's Most Intriguing Findings, from Barna Research Studies," December 12, 2000, www.barna.org.

3. See www.christianitytoday.com/leaders/newsletter/2005/cln50321.html.

4. See Pamela Binnings Ewen, *Faith on Trial* (Nashville, TN: Broadman & Holman, 1999).

5. Joan Windmill Brown, *Every Knee Shall Bow* (Old Tappan, NJ: Fleming H. Revell, 1978), 160.